The
BEGINNING
and
THE END

The BEGINNING *and* THE END

Davida Coleman

Printed in the United States of America

ISBN 979-8-89114-152-0 (hc)
ISBN 979-8-89114-151-3 (sc)
ISBN 979-8-89114-153-7 (e)

Library of Congress Control Number: 2024925862

2025.03.31

MainSpring Books
5901 W. Century Blvd
Suite 750
Los Angeles, CA, US, 90045

www.mainspringbooks.com

DEDICATION

This book is the spoken word, in the form of poetry. This book tells a story of my life; the way I have been allowed to see, and depict it. As I have experienced my journey through life, I have realized that my joy is in acknowledging Christ. To Him, I give all honor, glory and praise. Thank you, God, for never giving up on me.

So many thanks to my three amazing children, whom God has truly blessed me with, for never having been a burden to me; not even for one day, ever. To my children, I leave my legacy of love. I know you will do great things in your lives, with the help of God, above.

THE BEGINNING AND THE END

Have you ever found yourself wanting to know
just how you ended up in a particular situation?

Or, why you were experiencing an emotion, or two,
that you'd rather not be experiencing?

Then you must ask yourself these questions:
When and where did everything start to fall apart?

Sometimes, you must go back
to the beginning,
to get to the end,
to find out where you are at now.

For myself, my question went something like this:
Where did my beginning lead?
And how did my end turn out to be so different
than what I would have expected for myself?

I've learned that although I've come across these words many times,
I've never really considered the thought of how the two words could,
would,
or if
they should
ever,
go together.

When you put the two words together you come up with an
oxymoron,
but when they stand alone,

they both serve two entirely different purposes;
taking on whole new meaning of their own. Each word
equivalent in meaning
as do the roles
that they play in or lives.

This having been said,
I know now that I plan on exploring these two words
throughout my life
until my beginning meets my end.
And, until I feel comfortable enough,
with not only myself,
but also feeling comfortable
and satisfied
with the answers that I find
to be acceptable
and true
for myself.

Because, I have learned this day, I cannot give up on myself;
because God has never once, ever, thought of giving up on me.
So, I must be worth more than I think of myself, this day.
And, I will continue to pray to God
to lead me down the road,
towards a righteous path.

I JUST WANNA SAY, THANK YOU

Thank you, Father, for these hands,
That do pray

Thank you, Father, for these feet
That do attempt to walk in a righteous way

Thank you for this heart
That You allow to feel both pleasure and pain

Thank you for this brain that you gave me
That lets me know I can
Face another day,
And, see my troubles through.

Thank you, for the wisdom to know:
Who gave me the grace and strength,
And who is always there for me,
Helping to pull me through.

JUBILEE

I listen to you and you give me answers.
I know all you want to do is speak to me,
but with all that I have and all that I am,
all that I want to do;
is...pull up a chair and make time for you,
and listen.

I listen to you,
and you show me the unbelievable.
I know that through your grace,
and in your name,
I can do all things,
because you strengthen me,
and it shall be done!

Although you answer to many names,
the name I know you by the best,
and the tongue you speak to me,
is the dialect I hear your voice in: Revelation.

Thank You, God,
for giving me this pair of eyes,
which allow me to see constant change.

GOD'S MAKING

God made many kinds of people
for many kinds of reasons.

He made different kinds of people,
so that those different kinds of people would speak about their
different experiences;
in hopes that...
"He whosoever shall have an ear, so then let them listen."

His purpose for those who would speak,
and for those who would have and ear;
that those people would all return to the same final resting place.

And That Their End,
Shall Be Their Beginning,
With all at home,
At the Foot of His Doorstep.

BIRTHRIGHT

Blessed but cursed,
because I'm made of flesh and at times it hurts.
I was created in his image- but fall short daily
cause I'm a product of a ready-made sinner. Street walker;
to teller of a fortune,
as usual, they've got me labeled all wrong.
I'm just a five-year-old girl with a prophetic calling.
As a child, I was giving you a message,
but it fell on deaf ears
'cause no one could receive it,
no one was there to believe it...

So then, you ask whose message was it anyway;
was it worth believing
or ever hearing in the first place?
It should have been 'cause God gave me the grace...

Blessed but cursed,
because of choosing God first;
over man, and all that man had to offer me.

Blessed but cursed;
after first deciding not to practice-
when we first practice to deceive;
Until I grew up, and stopped believing in God's love,
and adopted some of my own theories...

That maybe God didn't love me,
maybe all He wanted to do was sit on His throne, and judge me?
But that was only for one moment in my life,
in the blink of an eye.
Only a phase that I somehow allowed myself to go through;
before I would wake up and realize that this gift God gave me was
more than any man could ever imagine or define.
Yes. This gift is mine, and now I utilize it to its fullest all the time...

I believe that God does play jokes because after all, he uses me;
and that, in itself,
could be the joke entirely,
but the real joke is this: People fear me.
They fear this gift that was meant for the obvious-
to help me reveal who God is and how great His capability is.
But what's even worse than a person fearing me is- the fact that
some choose not to even believe. All I have to say is- "the Devil- the
all-time deceiver"!
So, now I've picked up this pen- and I'm talking to you about my eyes
and where they have been,
and how I got them...
Some might say that the gift of sight ain't nothin' to mess with
But, what I have to say about it is I wouldn't leave home one single day
without it!
It's my whole suit of armor for these days ahead
That some would deny me
That some might despise me
And that some would fear me
It's my birthright
And I make no apology
I accept it
Thank you, God, for this awesome blessing!

ROCK OF AGES

I was born in the year of sixty-six,
never stopped until now to give much thought over this.

Never gave much thought, as to who was around back then:
Who lived, who died, who were scholars.
Never saw myself taking the time out to break this down.

Time doesn't creep,
we just grow.

Time doesn't hold up,
we just move too slow.

Time doesn't show us a picture
too big
that we can't figure out
For some,
we just choose
to live in our own
little self.

Can't see beyond the things that we do see,
to see the things we need to see,
only seeing the things that we want to see.

We all have another side to us,
And, no, I'm talking about an alter ego,
what I'm speaking of is something mystical:
A side of our personality that most of us rarely enter into;
The side that helps our intellect grow.

We miss out on this,
simply because we're too busy blending,
living in the here-and-now,
missing out on everything that is surrounding us...
Like the gifts God gave us- and using them to be a blessing...

FIRST NEW SIGHT

The minute you are born you start to die;
but you are just a newborn, your eyes
are busy recording the sights
that they have never seen before.

Then you grow up to learn words like
fear,
pressure,
uncertainty,
dissatisfaction,
confusion
and
abandonment

And this is our preparation for the other side...

How soon do we have to live before we die?
How long do we have to live, before we learn that it's OK
To cry?
How long
do we have to try?

If we are fortunate enough, and given ample time,
is it possible to recapture our childhood again, if we desire?
Revisiting all of the moments in our lives,
that we once saw as significant moments,
to seek the answer to the questions
that we might have left behind?

How long will it take, before we are to know?
that it is the inevitable;
that we must grow.

What pair of eyes will we then be using,
when we start to make our journey back home?

Will they still be those same eyes
that fought so hard
and couldn't wait
to stay alive
to see what was to become of tomorrow?

VISIBLE IMAGE

Walking through the garden,
I looked up and saw an image that resembled a figure.

The figure was vague,
and appeared in the form of a shadow,
but from what I could see,
it seemed to be strong,
and had an image of peace upon its face.

I walked over to get a closer look,
and to make sure that my eyes weren't deceiving me.

As I approached the shadow-like image,
I noticed that there was something
Familiar
about this presence,
before me.

There was something about the scent of this image
that left an airy feeling in the seed of my soul,
so, I had to get one last glance,
as this image would soon turn and walk away.

That's when I saw
what was the reflection of
myself

"PEACE BE STILL"
was the whisper I heard,
as the shadow turned,
and walked off into the sunset,
with a smile on its face,
and the scent of a sweet, flowery, summer day,
that passed over.

COME HERE, CHILD

He came to me in a small house, at an age so tender; telling me...
I could do great things, because great things were in me.

He picked me up and showed me the way,
when my sight was that of a newborn.

He molded me,
like a piece of clay,
into a humble soul.

He laid his head on my shoulder,
and told me to worry no more,
because of what I had in store.

With his eyes, he showed me things
I never thought would be possible.

He told me to listen,
and listen closely,
for one day,
I would tell a story.

His voice was vague, but distinctively clear;
saying to me in an unconscious state,
"Always see through these pair of eyes,
that I have given to you."

Never look back,
always look forward,
and never doubt the steps
you have walked in.

Footprints in the sand
that you will leave behind
will only be the lessons
you have learned.

THE GIFT OF SIGHT

Being born with the gift of sight,
I write this stuff down now
In hopes that your struggle
No longer remains
That battle you fight:

I'm here to tell you:

That when you are troubled
And feeling down
That you don't have to drug up,
Or drug down, to find your way out.

That there is an alternative medicine
And to administer it
Will require of you, no doctor's visit.
Self-Help, will be all it takes
Call on The Lord
And he will restore that broken faith.

Remember, for every problem
There is always a solution.
We just must tap into it,
And for some of us this will mean
That we will have to change,
Or rethink, some thoughts.

And for some of us,
He would ask us to remember
That it is neither our right nor our privilege
To kill, steal or destroy.
It is an injustice against God,
and all His creation.

And as He, God,
and God alone,
Who sits on His throne,
Warns me to tell:

That if you have tried to do these things
That he has asked you not to do,
And even if you've committed
One or more of these acts,
And you feel that you have gotten away with them,
And no one has come for you...

Then God would have you to know
That society will not only find you out,
And that they will shut,
and lock,
The door on,
and behind you.
And throw away the key.

Because unlike God,
Society is not as forgiving,
And can be harsh at times.
Even cruel.

Losing sight of the fact that
Jesus had a mission.
And now it's left up to us.
It is our job, as his people
To see it through.

But just as you have taken
And made light of that same fact,
When you committed one of those acts,
Failing to realize that Jesus died for you,
And that he came
So that you may have life

Now you find yourself,
Stuck:
Same position as your punisher.
Now, you must find a way to forgive them, as they must forgive you.

But when the world starts to shut down,
And tries to completely void you out,
God will be there,
to help you figure it all out.

< 18 >

TESTIMONIAL

No house without electricity
could make me feel disconnected

No house without lights
could take my sight

No house without water
could wash away my soul

No house without food
could stop Jesus from feeding me courage to overcome

No house without a structure or support
could stop the visions God gave me

No lack of knowledge that the Devil would try to rob
could keep me from doing the job that God has appointed me to do

To go and tell his people that he is real,
I know, because of what I once came from

That no Devil could ever be greater than God;
God just allows him to exist,
So that we may choose life over evil,
Beating the devil at his own trick

So that God could one day look down at us
And be pleased at what he sees in us,
That our smile is the very image of his heart
And that we have overcome defeat

MY REVELATION;
TO THE FISHERMAN'S DREAM

Father,
I Thank God for giving me this set of parents,
and these sets of circumstances for me to embrace,
and I do mean
embrace.

To enrich my life and character,
so that if nothing else is ever made good
of this set of tragic circumstances.
I can carry with me these unforgettable experiences;
using them to breathe a fresh, new outlook on my life,
indeed,
from here on out.

And operating with full authority by you,
Father God,
to reach out and touch the lives
of as many as possible.
Father, you alone allow me to bring the good news:
that there is light in, and after the darkest hour.
And in our darkest hour,
it is you only Father God who never leaves our side;
or leaves us unable to do your bidding,
to the point of completion.

I sit here today,
to share this complete story,
and to confirm that the will of God shall be done.
And although I am not completed yet...

I am a project in the making,
And a work-in-progress.

A FISHERMAN'S DREAM

Being born black
Wasn't half the problem
I was about to have.
Might have been one of my first
But I got over that.

The ghetto didn't embrace me.
I embraced it.
And all the mentality
That went along with it.
If I hadn't
Then I probably wouldn't have ever sat down
To write this.

As the song goes, "Papa may have been a rolling stone,
Wherever he laid his hat was his home"
So, I learned early on from my dad
That home could be wherever you're at.

From the family down the street
Who shared their dad with me,
To the next-door neighbors,
On both sides of my fence...

From being locked out after school,
Too small to climb through a window.
So, I did the next best thing
And headed next door
To receive some shelter.

And while I was there
My friend's mom used to make this bread.
I remember how fast she
Used to knead that dough,
And bake that bread.
Can still smell it now.

All pipin' hot,
Fresh out of the oven,
Just like time hasn't moved anywhere.
Only I did.
And on the opposite side of that fence,
Was always the smell of fresh fish.
I remember as a child being told the parable of Jesus,
And how he fed many men, women and children,
With just five loaves of bread and two fish.
That's how I felt about my neighbors,
Thank God, for Jesus's people, who continued to do his will.

And the fisherman' s wife?
Let's just say that she was an angel in disguise,
As she fed me milk and cookies plenty of times.
The touch of her hand so kind and gentle,
Took me away for a moment in time,
To a peaceful place.
Letting me know.
in the only way that she knew how:
Having never had a child herself.
That God takes care of his own,
And in the end, it would be all right.

Around the corner from our house,
Lived the fisherman's friend,
Who fed me lunch and told me stories,
Taking me away to places
That were far away and unknown to me.
But as a young child,
I remember enjoying listening to them,
He took me on a journey that with a ticket I couldn't buy,
But in my mind,
I was already there.

But enough about travel.
Let's journey back to reality,
And where I really lived.

My first memory of home
Was that of a baby and learning to walk.
After that, it all seemed crazy
My dad would hit my mom,
Only to be taken to jail,
Where he'd be held for some time...
Only to return to the start and completion of another cycle

But that seemed to get old
So, Dad feeling trapped inside,
himself,
Now had to find another way out.
So, dad stepped up his game,
And found other pleasures to keep him at home,
But those turned out to be the lives of two innocent souls.

< 24 >

As if drinking and beating wasn't enough,
He had to go and place his hands where a father should not ever touch.
Although it didn't happen to me,
I was to be considered one of the lucky three.
Then again, I was right there.
Left in the middle to see.
So, then you ask yourself:
Who's the lucky one?
Was it really me?

Because Dad always needed someone to talk to.
About life and his dirty little deeds.
Again, I became the lucky one.
To explain life through the eyes of a child,
To a grown man,
That seemed to have a passion
To please the Devil.
As if those same pair of eyes hadn't already seen enough;

I would now become the one
To teach this man some lessons.
Out of the mouth of a babe,
With intellect that should have been small,
I told the man about what I saw,
And that it was wrong.
He smirked at me,
As if something were funny.
And at that moment,
For the first time in my short-lived life,
That's when I knew that God existed!

And although my Dad felt as if he was escaping justice
I knew then, that God would punish-
And although I was only a child,
And although my Dad did some rotten things,
I couldn't help but feel more sorrow for him
Than my heart would allow my own two sisters;
Because the strong can and will survive.
But who would be there for my Dad
When he finally begins to break down,
and cries?

Drama,
Drama,
Drama.
That's the world I lived in.
But that's my sister's story,
And partially mine,
But my story goes on.
With Mama and Daddy's scars
That he left on mama' s abused mind.

The Cost I Counted Up Here;
I Would Pay a High-Fine.
I don't know if it was because I was the last child,
out of five,
Or if it was because I was born the last girl,
And was the last hope of bringing mama a baby boy into this world.
Was it because I befriended a man,
A Dad,
That I knew that I could never have?
Putting aside those things;
That he did to my mom and my sisters.
So that I could feel like
I lived in a home,
And not just a house.

Whatever the case may be,
Something terrible went wrong in that house.
And instead of me turning out to be that blessing from the skies,
that mama sure could have had used,
I became instead the child that mama abused.
I became the child transparent,
Out of sight,
Because it always felt like to me
Like mama couldn't stand the sight of me.
So, again, early on,
I learned to make myself disappear.
Talking to, and spending time with, God,
When no one else was near or could hear.

Maybe I was being punished
For having ever even listened
to Dad,
In the first place.
Because after all,
Wasn't that the wife's place?
But how could Mama possibly do this for Dad?
When Dad seemed to take so much pride
In oppressing Mama's spirit?
The same type of pain that I soon too would experience.

But, I don't blame Mama now for any of that,
Because who could have ever known,
To what extent,
That Mama would, and did, suffer through?
The part that I struggled with,
And for a long time couldn't forgive Mama for,
Until I picked up this pen,
And started writing it down,
Doing some of my own listening to self...
Wasn't the part where Mama started beating me

For any little reason;
Outside, inside, it really didn't matter
You pick the place, and reason,
And I was probably beaten for it.

From Mama being aggravated
And upset that Dad wasn't around,
To mama having a bad day at work,
To mama merely being mad at one of my siblings;
Meant I was probably gone catch hell.
But keep in mind,
I forgive Mama for all of that.

Even when it got to the point where it hurt physically,
From the beatings with belts, twigs, hands,
or whatever else Mama could find.
Nothing hurt worse than the Mother that I could never find.

Growing up,
I felt unattached at the seams,
At the root of my soul.
So, I grew up with the dream
Of making some place my home.
That is why I visited all those neighbors
I spoke of earlier,
My search started early on in life;
Looking for a place
I could call my home.
Now, I have three children of my own, and I pray to God that I have
broken the cycle,
And given them a home.

IT IS IN THE TAKING OF THE WHOLE TRUTH, THAT THE WHOLE MAN LIVES

What pours out of my soul is no different then what pours out of yours, I just keep a record of mine, so that I can complete my goal

I look at life through these eyes and wonder if at some point in time; won't we all be held accountable for our sins?

They say it's not a sin unless it feels like it is, to me at times it feels like a whole and I'm burning inside, deep within

These eyes have seen a lot, they have seen time change, places change and yet certain things still remain the same

Very little, to no peace to been seen on city streets, the hungry still remain unfed, the cost of living still rising while very few make ends meet-barely surviving. The young and the old still sharing the same story that war times still near, the absence of God- but Christianity everywhere

The do-gooder' s few and far between, while the rich line their pockets on the poor man's dream. The harsh reality of it all is that one day, somehow, some way- we will all stand in judgment; we will all be accountable for our brothers' fall

We can't move past, until we move forward and we can't move forward until we know who or what drives us, moves us on and gives us the will, the imagination, the intellect to deal with this all

Is it the impossible to believe for one moment, that God is still on the throne, and truth be told that he has never left us alone, and that one day he's bringing all of his children back home?

WHEN WE FIRST PRACTICE TO DECEIVE

I can only identify with the pain inside,
my memory is long as the day,
my memory is my own personal history,
my memory is relevant.

From identifying with the first type of pain daddy caused,
from just not being there showing up for my cause,
to the good-bye's until I see you next times,
my pain is relevant.

Never new growing up that I'd learn so much,
never new growing up that this would all means so much,
never new growing up that daddy without ever even trying
to take shape of me would mold me.

Growing up, my Daddy, to me, was my everything,
but then again, Daddy couldn't stand there long enough,
couldn't finish the job he'd started,
couldn't see me through to the end.

So then it goes on, to man a boy,
who became my toy,
but soon to follow tears of joy,
yea, this story just like the first...
didn't last long,
just like daddy...
boy meets girl.

But that's alright,' cause to this very day,
all I know and all I've learned is that man is man,
and I no longer see myself as that little girl.

And, that the Father I now know
is the only real Father a girl could ever want.

Thank You, God!

FAILING TO CHECK WITH GOD

Sometimes we let our parents make decisions for us, about our lives;
Not even knowing that for many of us, it is our own reality that we must live with.
That our parents were, and, or are, just as messed up and confused;
If not more, than we are.
This is OK to say out loud.
Because by saying this stuff out loud; it gives us the strength that we need...
To mend some broken areas in our lives, and give back the junk to its rightful owner,
Whoever that may be?
And besides it's our reality, our everyday life...
So why fight the truth, why not embrace it?
And by doing so, turn yourself from failure into success
And if this does not pertain to you
Know that you are not only blessed, but also very fortunate!

Often, we don't find all this stuff out
that we have been carrying around
Until it seems to be too late
And because of that one time that you listened to them
You may have played a joint part, in confusing your own judgment,
by listening to them You feel like you may have destroyed your life
But something inside you told you to listen to them
That, somehow, they must have known what they were talking about
Otherwise, why did they speak the will of themselves, into our lives?

I guess the lesson here is:
At times, humans can and do fail, they fail both you and I
They fail, because of the way they were raised

They fail, because they pretended to be something that they're not
They fail, because the generation before them, raised them, and they failed, too...

They fail, because they fail, simply because they choose to...
They fail, because they failed to check with God.
So, Now I've learned from all my failures,
To Trust in God,
And, to check in with Him first!

BREATHE A POSITIVE WORD INTO YOUR LIFE

We breathe life
Into our every word
Words allow us
To have a beginning and an end
Our first words
Were the names of
The first people we knew
And for me I can't say
It was mom or dad
Because you can't claim
What you've never had
We use them as we need them
And we remember them as we need them
It was words that your parents
Breathed you into life with
And gave you a name
And when you were a baby
It was your parents' words
That you learned to cling to
It was a state of mind
That walked you into
A state of depression
But it was words
That carried you out of it
Back into the right frame of mind
It is words that we use
When we hurt one another
By name calling
And it is words that we use

When we choose to make up
With the ones we love
And desire their forgiveness
Words can hurt
Words at times make no sense
Words can embrace
And words can release us
And it is through the thought of our words
That the devil can be allowed in
Words can lead us
To seek the truth
The way and the life
That is how we end up in Churches
Praying to God.

THE MEANING OF LIFE:
THE WAY I SEE IT

This life is a contest, and I'm a winner.
I can't lose, because I know who's in control of my life.
And, he's also a winner.
He's fail-proof.
This life is a concert, and I'm gonna go through it singing my song.
This life is church, and I've already made my confession.
This life is Art, and with the help of God, I'm gonna write it,
like Picasso saw it.
This life is Culture, and I'm in the melting pot.
Living in the best and worst of times,
But I still know I'm blessed.
This life is hell on earth at times, but I still see heaven through it.

THE DREAM I HAVE

I have a dream, and I think it's the same as God's;
That one day, all poverty would end, and faith would fill the void.

I have a dream that there is life after death, and that this concept
could be passed along; giving us all the substance of strength, that
which we need to carry on.

I have a dream that every un-rested soul could find peace, and that
the owner of that peaceful soul, would go out into the world, and
create more.

I have a dream of testifying for God; of going out into the world to
share with others, of what he has done in my life, in hopes that others
might feel compelled, and catch on.

I have a dream that people would stop thinking small, and remember
that God can do it all.

All things are possible through Christ Jesus, who strengthens.

I have a dream that charity would not be through a selection process
That it shall be; that every man shall prosper.

I have a dream of living to see the day that no matter where I go, I
will feel the presence of the Lord, through his people's face.

I have a dream that all the sick and infirmed, depressed, oppressed, young and old, healthy, wealthy, educated and un-educated, the upper-class, working class, and middle-class, the poor, and every race, and denomination, all receive their blessings from God. Blessings that they so rightfully deserve; that have their name on each and every one of them.

And, that no blessings get marked "Return to Sender", because they refused to acknowledge the address, as marked.

WORKING THROUGH SOME THINGS

Too afraid to go to sleep and dream,
for you're afraid you might have to wake up to reality,
and deal with what you have seen.

But what do you do, once your awake?
Do you stay that way?
For some of us we sleep-walk,
creep,
creep,
creeping,
over the things that we've just seen.
Past,
Present,
Future.
Trying to figure out what that was all about that we just saw
Was that me, who was dreaming those things?
Or, was that me thinking up those things?
Or, was that just my imagination having fun with me?
How do I know if I could hardly see?
Lastly, I knew, I was just sleeping.
Or was I just thinking?
Maybe I was daydreaming, while I was standing to my feet?

ROCK-A-BY-LULLABY

Got issues on this side,
so I take them with me, to the other side.
Put them to sleep with me,
in hopes that I might be able to get an analogy.
Just like the TV set;
I let it run all night to put me to sleep,
in hopes that my brain might do the same
Run all night long...
To give me answers for which I long.
Whether I work it out here, or I work it out there,
what's the difference?
As long as I see,
The last issue on your mind is what you'll probably work out,
while you're out.
But, what if your sleep becomes your everyday thing?
What am I talking about?
Go to sleep sometime,
And try it...
You will find out...

THE SKIN I'M IN

They say it's our suit of armor, but is it, really?
Deceitful as it may be, it is my very own package.
Beautiful; it can be, if I choose to let it shine.

I dress it up, I take it out,
I carry it around with me,
but several times it has let me down.
Beautiful it can be, if I allow it to be.

Scented perfume helps me discard its weakening state
that at times has failed me.
I bathe it, and oil it, in hopes that it will sparkle and glimmer,
while all the while, I know I must cleanse out the inside, first.

Yet and still, I continue to carry it around
like a weighted package,
and it continues to turn against me
with every footstep measured;
until I can receive my final cleansing.

WHO SHALL I BECOME?

Angry,
resenting all that is a symbol,
and that resembles life exists.

Disturbed
by the fact
that time moves on,
and waits for no one.

Countless times
I have tried to enter a place of peace,
but peace just wouldn't have me;
instead fear and shame embraced me.

I keep looking around
and wondering if and when
someone
will ever notice
me,
for who I really am.

I wait for the day
that I will be given the chance
to release what has been trapped inside me.

And, I live for the day
that I find that complete being;
the one that I never thought
I could become.

I CRY OUT TO YOU, O LORD!

If it is not meant to be,
then let me long no more.

Take away this gaping hole in my heart,
and replace it with whatever is right.

Let me know what I am to do,
in that hour of need.

Give me strength to face defeat,
if it is defeat which I must have.

Move this process along,
so I can have what is rightfully my own;

and peace of mind,

at last.

Hear my cry, O, Lord!

WHY I CRY OUT TO YOU: BECAUSE I KNOW YOUR NAME!

Why I cry out to you,
because my heart longs for you to take away the pain,
and fill my cup with a substance so pure.

My flesh cries out to you,
because of guilt stricken pain,
caused from the drunkenness of willful misconduct.

Yet and still,
it continues to burn,
like a torch in the night.

Sin is all around me,
and I can't seem to shake it,
so this is when I stop and call out to you;

"Be merciful!"
I beg of you;
for I know your name.
But my body carries
a weighted package,
that keeps me in shame.

Hear my pleas, hear my cries,
O Lord, that you will wipe these tears, and one day,
I will be able to see with a pair of dry eyes.

GRANT ME STRENGTH

Carry me over in my times of need,

To the visible side of where I can see

All the things that I can be.

Take me to a time and place,

Where I no longer lack my dignity and grace.

Bless me, Lord, with the things that I must know.

Grant me strength; help me grow.

GRANT ME ONE WISH

Grant me one wish, Lord: that I may stay simple and true.

Keep me purified, and cleansed, in truth.

Bathe me with your wisdom and knowledge,

That every fight may not be my struggle.

Keep your hands on and over me.

Keep my eyes on your eyes.

Let me stay focused on the blessings and visions that you have sent to me.

At the end of each day, Lord, keep me whole.

INCOMPLETE SOUL

Black places, clouded faces, visions of dreams left behind;
burned in my mind, of a place and time when everything was mine.

Now, all I have left is my mind, that sits here and does nothing, but play tricks on me.

Who loves me?

Who is to be loved?

And, how long must I wait, until it can all be mine?

Time now plays tricks on me, and leads me towards curiosity.

Time plays tricks on me; and leaves my body and soul scared and tired.

Time plays tricks on my head; telling me this issue is old, and I am all of half-dead.

The Devil plays tricks with my mind; telling me to open up a box of salt...
because he is about to get serious with me,
and add that salt to my open wounds;
wounds that are already bleeding.

The Devil plays tricks with my mind, so that I won't achieve my personal best.

The Devil plays with my mind, simply because I let him!

GREAT EXPECTATIONS

Trying so hard to do the right thing.
Trying to live well is when
I failed
to succeed.

But, if I set expectations
of myself,
high above society,
I am sure to fail.

If I meet myself somewhere in the middle,
between success and failure,
then I feel like I have not filled the void.

But, when I set expectations of myself that are attainable,
and I let go of all my cares in and of the world,
that is when I am blooming;
blossoming,
in to a marvelous creation.

GOD KNOWS I CRY

Pain is pain.
Mine can't be compared to yours.
But who's to say
That mine is less than,
Equal to,
Or greater than yours?
And, no pain could compare to the pain
That we caused Jesus Christ.

There's pain for love,
Pain for loss,
Pain for knowledge,
And, simply learning life's truth.
Pain for error,
And pain for never even trying
Or caring.

For some,
The greatest pain that they will experience is
The pain of understanding who we really are;
Because with this pain,
We accept some truth.
And, what we do with these truths
Is totally up to us.

Pain is an illusion, to distract us,
That the Devil tripped over,
And stumbled onto,
And that he now keeps on using against us,
To help him keep us stuck.

But remember, the next time you're in pain,
Who's waiting for you on the other side.
He feels pain too.
His pain is in the tears you cry.

GOD WILL BE ON TIME

I'm sorry
if I met you in the wrong place
in time.
But it's only because
God planned it that way.

Would have stayed if I could,
but who would have known,
who could have known,
way back then...
That God would have used those circumstances
way back then,
to build Him a man.

I traveled through so many thoughts and
Got stuck so many places...
But in the end, it would be God who would pull me through...
Because it was meant for me to be used.

And I'm sorry
if we met at the wrong place
in time,
But who could have known,
who should have known,
back then,
that God would be on time.

ONE COMPLETE SOUL

I will become many things, on my road to success.

I will become a dreamer, a person of vision, with the images inside my head.

I will become a poet, with words to paper, with pen.

I will become a climber of high peaks, on a road uphill, towards success.

I will become a listener; a person of fewer words, with purpose that lay ahead.

I will become the owner of one complete soul.

THROUGH IT ALL

Things that should come easy to us, don't.

Words that we should say, we won't.

We speak when someone listens,

but what if he or she won't?

Do we shut down our speech;

or do we try and reach?

Do we cast aside, and never look back?

Or, do we try and help them get back on track?

The next time you're faced with one of these adversities that life has

dealt to you, ask yourself if...

Will you rise to the occasion, and meet the challenge?

THAT WHICH DOESN'T KILL YOU, MAKES YOU STRONGER

Been studying life too long,
and all the how's and why's.
I've been paying attention to all the wrong things;
To the people I've come in contact with.
And to how I've been treated wrong;

Never stopping to think for one moment,
That it was me who had it all wrong.
That those experiences were stories.
And those stories were lessons
That would one day soon be told.
Just what I needed to make me strong.

I had some disappointments in life,
Some early on.
The loss of a man, who was never a dad.
The loss of affection from a mother, and her protection.
To the loss of a man to call my own;
That I could possibly love...

So then,
I have experienced my fair share of hurt.
But not more than enough.
Because after all,
the Man in Charge doesn't give to us
More than we can bear.

He expects us to pick up the pieces,
And move on with our life, and story,
To share our experiences along the way.
So that we can be the example that He has made.

LIKE A MOTH TO A FLAME

Why is it that some of us get stuck, and some of us move on?

How is it that only some of us receive our blessings,

and others refuse to accept them?

Is it because our past haunts us,

or is it that we haunt ourselves,

with trouble that we get caught up into?

Can we remove the curse from our lives,

or is it ourselves,

who give fuel to the flames?

Can I ever learn to remember that?

That the past is just the past?

THE PATH

Why must I walk a path that has already been chosen for me?
Might it be easier for me to live my life, as a reflection of me?
Or, is it possible that this reflection of myself is truly the spirit that
walks the path, instead of my feet?

If it's movement you ask for, and it is movement I give to you,
through my mistakes I have made,
then surely this is enough to open up the gates of Heaven.

What is all too confusing; is all a bit much...

I can only wait, and wonder if my all was enough...

Longing to seek the approval of your merciful grace,
I will walk the face of Earth, with composure and grace.

For, when it comes the time and hour for me to exit this place,
I can only hope that my life would have been example enough,
and all lessons, in my chapter book, have no blank space.

SHIPWRECKED

Emotions can be the vessel
That leads us into a shipwreck,
In the middle of the night.

It is by our own nature,
That which we fear the unknown,
Which allows us to then
Feel the pressures of the world.
And, attached to those pressures comes
More uncertainty of the unknown.

Situations in our lives that seem confusing,
And that seem to make no sense at all;
Those are the times
When we seem to function at our best.

Because if life never shows us the unfair,
And we never experienced
Some type of despair,
Then how would we know,
Or ever be sure, that God was there?
Right in the midst of those things,
And that He did care?

Fear,
Pressure,
Uncertainty,
Dissatisfaction,
Confusion,
Abandonment...

Emotions such as these
Give us reasons to thank God,
And for us to get down on our knees.
For if we are always standing,
And seldom kneeling,
Then we certainly cannot be
too appealing to God.

And if all those emotions aren't
Reason enough for you to talk to God,
Then what you need to remember is
That every failure is our success story,
Turned inside out.

And that God planned it that way;
As he makes no mistakes, have no doubt.

ACCOUNTABLE FOR MY OWN ACTIONS

An accurate account of my life,
should it be told,
is that I have humbled myself;
consumed in loss and refrained from shame.

But, truth be told,
I have tried to fight the good fight,
and have fallen short,
for sin.

Humbled, yes.
At times;
but only until stubborn pride
seeps in.

Consumed by restless,
sleepless nights,
which I fight when the Devil comes,
to try and steal my sight.

Somehow,
God always knows
just how much food I'm in need of,
for my soul,
and restores it all;
giving me the tools that are necessary
to complete my goal.

FATHER KNOWS BEST

I could have been lost to the streets.

I could have been the one that God never got the chance to know.

I could have been bought and sold,
and bought again,
but the Lord I know
bestowed mercy,
upon my soul.

I could have been ugly,
Well,
was ugly,
but could have stayed that way,
until the Lord touched me.

I could have been dirty,
without a washing,
but instead,
the price of my head
had been purchased long ago.

Guess He always knew
that He would have to allow all roads to lead home,
and that the path that I had chosen for myself
would lead me to the foot of his doorstep;
with a crown of thorns placed upon my own forehead,
having been placed there
by myself.

Guess He always knew
that His mercy and grace
would have to follow me
from this day forward,
because I would fall short of Him,
from the weight of my own sins.

Guess He always knew me,
even when I didn't know myself,
and thought I did.

Thank You, Father,
For Always Knowing What's Best!

TROUBLED, NO MORE

Comfortably,
I sit with troubles, no more.
That all is fine now,
and all shall be done.

Through the Grace of God,
I awake each day,
and give thanks to Him
for another chance
to rectify my wrongs,
and a second chance
at becoming stronger.

If time should run out
before I get to the finish line,
I could only say,
"I have come,
I have seen,
and have given my all!"

POVERTY

Once upon a time,
I lived in a place
called poverty and despair.
But, then I learned why
I was dwelling there.

Because poverty can mean
many different things
I got stuck,
and almost held up
there.

If the poverty you think
I'm speaking of is money,
if that's your trouble,
then give it to God.
He's a multiplier.
He can give you
double
for your trouble.

But, if you think
that the poverty I'm speaking of
is addressed to your mind,
you're absolutely right.
Our mind was not created
only to be confined.
Our thoughts should never be
allowed to remain constricted.

Your thoughts
could very well
end up becoming your meal ticket.

So, don't get stuck on the simple stuff,
and lose thought of sight.
Remember that Jesus died for both you and I,
And because of this,
we no longer have to pay the price.

Remember,
this thing that we call life;
at times,
we're all guilty,
of letting it beat us down.

Remember that this battle was fought
many a year, and many a times ago.
And, many James, John, and Lukes lived,
And Saul's, turned to Paul's.

Walked this same walk for us.
The same walk that many of us,
today,
feel that we are walking.
And, they made it through;
to the other side of despair,
to hope.

In hopes,
that we might do the same.
I know there are a lot of things
that we must remember,
but here's one more
thing for you to consider:

That the battle you're fighting
Is only half of your story;
You just have not yet walked
in your glory.

No,
none of us should live
in poverty or despair,
because God is
the Ultimate Battery Repairer.
Call on Him,
in your hour of need.
And he'll show up.
I guarantee!

Jump-starting you;
from the place in which you broke-down.
Giving you a fresh new start,
from there on out.

Poverty is the inability to see yourself through.

OH, HAPPY DAY!

Making a move out of poverty into sanity.
with quality, not quantity.
Writing an autobiography,
of all things, I'm allowed to see.
Keeping a scrapbook for memory.

A sane man said:
"The healthier, the wealthier, the wiser",
and "A mind is a terrible thing to waste",
but what really needs to be considered,
in the here and now,
is the Love of God's grace;
and its entirety.

It's not something that we need to consider,
or to be contemplated over.
it's something that he gives to all of us.
That's just the way it is.
But some of us never give much thought to this.
Or worse, never know it exists...
Because they refuse to give the credit to Him,
For all that He is.
So then, what knowledge is power,
If we the people are left powerless?

Never opening their eyes
to allow his light to shine down on them,
so that they may capture that moment,
with the perfect photograph
of that "Oh, Happy Day!":

When they first learn of His grace!

ON MY KNEES

Because I know that I am not to pleasing to God,
if I'm always standing
Because of this knowledge,
I'm in church every opportunity given;
kneeling and praying to God.

Yes, I can pay my respects to Him,
In my time spent,
while I'm in the confinement
of my own home.

But it is God's choice,
that I stop by His house,
to pray for all lost souls.
And for all of who don't know
the power of prayer.

I pray for the family member
that we all know and have,
That refuses to give God
all they have.

I pray for those who refuse to allow
God entry into their homes and hearts.
So that he can open up His heart to them;
And one day his home will be the very place,
that they can call their own.

I pray to God,
thanking Him
for saving my life, ...so long ago.

Helping me to keep my soul intact,
and leading me into Glory,
Where I can and will be crowned with my gold

We only have-not, because we ask not.

AND, THE CHILD
SHALL LEAD THE WAY

I knew a girl,
Who tried real hard
To always do the right things
With not having much to go on.
She created much to work off of.
She had a set of parents,
Who for whatever reasons
Took separate lives.

But her mom
Would meet another man,
Who was willing to step in, though,
And finish the job...
That her dad didn't want...
But at times could play the part.

She. could have ended up
Confused,
But instead,
She put all her circumstances together;
To make good of
What seemed to be a bad start.

It must have been hard for her
To trust the man
Who would end up raising her,
Because up until that point,
All she knew
Was Mama who raised her.

But, she quickly embraced this man,
As if he were her natural father.
Maybe because
That's all she ever wanted;
Another side of herself,
That didn't resemble mama's face,
But that she could love,
As she did Mama, equally.

Her Mom and Dad
Never really had to teach her much.
It's as if she was already here before.
And, now ready to help out,
And do her part.

She took sick a few times,
And almost scared Mama half-to-death.
But, I guess
That's what Mama
Needed to go through, with her,
To find her special blessing,
Because at that point
In Mama's life,
When Mama gave birth to this child,
Mama was barely fighting
To save her own life~
Failing to thrive.

But, God knows our every need,
Before we ever need it.
God knew.
That Mama needed something
To snap her out of that depression.

< 73 >

So, He sent her the best gift
That he could:
He sent her that baby girl
An awesome blessing!

Now, this child
Is almost ready to fly on her own.
And Mama wonders
If they both can make it on their own.

Because,
For so long
They have grown together.
But, God will let no man do them under.
As He has joined them together, forever
"God so loved the world,
That he gave his only begotten Son."

Nothing is more precious to me,
In my life,
Than my child's love for me,
And my God above,
Who I give all the praise.

THANKS FOR MY CHILD

I looked up one day,
And didn't have to even look in the mirror,
Because the child standing in front of me
Was that image.

Then God spoke to me saying,
"You always wondered
What your life would have looked like,
And how it would have turned out,
If you would have only done the right things;
The things I asked of you."

That's when I knew,
That that child was not only the blessing I needed,
But that God was showing me something.

With hopes like my own,
And dreams the same,
I can only sit here and wait to see,
What God has created,
In the image of me.

I know my own relationship with God is personal,
But He just always keeps on showing me how great He is!

Who would have ever had thought
That we love our children,
Because they are the hope and dream,
That so many of us have lost?
And, that it is not through them
That we live vicariously,
But it is because of them that we live at all!

< 76 >

BASTARD CHILD

From the time I'm conceived, I don't know my own name.
That decision, like many others, will be determined for me.
Every parent wants you to believe, and know, that you were
conceived in love.
But, for every rule, there is an exception to be made.
Some parents conceive a child, but never accept the child that they
bore.
Never to grasp how they were conceived...
Or the parenting concepts they were to follow ...
But the child was conceived in love?
Can't wait so much as...as long as...I'm only one day old...
Before he turns tail, and runs.
And now, I have no last name, to call my own.
Hopefully, Mama can remain sane long enough, to give me her last
name.
But, that was my start, and very much of my past.
That's who the world perceived me to be, but I know differently.
Thanks to God; to the Man Above.
They say that God doesn't make mistakes.
Then, why is the world so quick to judge?
But, my story gets better, and even has a happy ending.
I went through the water, and received the best blessing that a Father
could give a child.
I received the truth that shall set me free:
That I've always belonged to God.
Man only played a small part, in the creation of me.
Now, I have the same Father as the whole, wide world,
And many brothers and sisters, to walk through life with,
The way God always planned it;
All along.

IF YOU HAVE NOTHING GOOD TO SAY, THEN SAY NOTHING AT ALL

People will try to tell you
That His words are only our thoughts.

And, at times
It is our thoughts, who speak to us.

Don't be fooled by these words,
Because this is not the Message.

Words are our thoughts,
And our thoughts are the Message
That will carry us from the beginning to the end.
If we let them.

People will make you feel,
Or try to tell you that it is you,
And you alone,
Functioning off your own selfish needs.

That God has nothing,
Or very little,
to do with you.
Your want, or your need,
And that it is your own greed,
Driving you,
from deep within.

Ask yourself that question?
Then examine from within!
If it doesn't apply to you,
Then, shake it off,
And get back to the business of pleasing Him,
And what He created you for,
Knowing who's in control of your every thought.

Continue to do His will
Because much is needed.
So, then much shall be done.

As you move towards what is rightfully yours,
Know that it has already been promised to you!

Never mind those people who would rather see you quiet,
Because your actions will speak louder than words,
And they won't be spoken softly:

To God be the glory!

WHOEVER HAVE AN EAR, SO THEN SHALL HE LISTEN

They say that it is the eyes that are the window and pathway to the human soul,

But often I find that it is through the ear that the story can be told.

The Bible tells us that "he so-whoever have an ear, so then shall he listen"...

If your volume is never turned up; so then how will you listen?

He speaks to us through many different thoughts, forms and ways,

But through the volume of the ear, His voice is never vague...

As a baby, you first start to speak when you hear your first sounds

In Christianity, similarity can be found...

You first start to listen, when you first remember His name

Not a minute before will you have an ear for His call...

He speaks to many and it's quite possible that He can speak to all

But only if you allow Him, will He give you a call...

Just as the eye has a job to carry the soul, the ear plays a vital part in renewing our heart...

So, the next time you receive a long-distance call, and you hear nothing from the other end, don't assume there's no one there on the receiving end...

Don't hang up. Just say hello and speak clearly to who is listening In...

Once you have your volume up, and running, remember; like a furnace, in the dead-middle of winter:

Never to shut it off...

Once you have your volume up and functioning at a capacity, that only you can hear, to give it proper maintenance, keep it tuned into the exact channel that it was to which it was turned, when you first received that message, so clear...

To receive proper updates on your future, and what's in store.

Thanking God, for ever having created something far more advanced and greater than mankind- with technology, could ever had thought up.

< 81 >

WHAT IS FAITH?

You only trust Me when it's convenient for you to come My way.

I told you I was preparing you for the next step of the way.

The answers that you receive from Me might not always be to your

liking, but they're the ones that are necessary to be handed down,

so that one day you might receive a crown.

My answers to your questions are not made nor meant to be riddles.

Just as your questions you ask of me are neither silly, or ridiculous.

Just as My mere presence in your life should be more than sufficient.

I give you life; I should be more than enough.

Yes, it's true that you sometimes run low on faith,

Because you are made of flesh, and I have created you that way.

But, the next time you are given a test,

pay attention to the lesson,

because you just might receive a blessing.

WILL

"Will"
is our ability to see ourselves
through any situation,
with the help of God.
It is not, by the legal term defined;
A document,
by which a person directs
his or her estate
to be distributed upon death;
also termed "testament".
Legal terminology also uses these words:
Will.
Desire.
Choice.

But, it does not stop there,
it goes on
Will, to be defined by God's legal terminology,
is something He has desired all of us to have.
Praying for us that we will use this gift,
that He has graciously given us,
to make the choices that we must;
by running all our ideas,
troubles and thoughts, by Him, first!

So then, after realizing the power of will
Ask yourself the question:
What have you willed
into the meaning and purpose
of your own life?

And was it all with the help of,
And compared and matched too, the will of God?
If your will and effort can allow you to see the reflection of God
In the choices you've made,
Then good!

Congratulate yourself,
because you have utilized your gift
Just as God would have wanted for you.
but if your answer falls short,
not to worry,
because you can always go back to the place
where you feel you started to go wrong.
Tell God about it.
And then repent; ask God for forgiveness, and invite Him in.
And He will show up, that's another gift he's given to us, His
guarantee.

Because it is God's testament to His people;
that He will not enter in,
Until we ask Him to.

So, from this day forward,
Let it be by His will, and not your own.
That you desire Him to lead your life
in the direction that He would have it go for you.
So that you know that you have made
the right choices in your life,
By having chosen God over all else,
first and foremost, in your life.

< 84 >

EVERYTHING IN MODERATION

Let me break it down for you, the best way that I can:
Work,
rest,
food,
and play:
All this given to us,
in a twenty-four-hour day.
And out of those twenty-four hours,
we then break it down once more,
Leaving us left with twelve left, to fill the void,
From sun up, to sun down,
We work hard to accomplish our daily tasks,
But God has provided us a plan of attack.
To make sure that we accomplish our all,
What you must do for yourself, this day,
Is ask yourself this question;
How much time are you spending on each?
Let's start with work, a six to eight-hour workday.
With breaks to eat in between.
Leaves us four hours left of daylight,
to do with what we wish.
But it's the before and after hours,
that God's concerned with.
Do we wake up at the start of each day,
giving our thanks?
And after we have done all that we can do,
to complete the daily need?
Who is it that we recognize, before we close our eyes,
and fall fast asleep?

And if many of you are spending more
than six to eight hours at work,
and are working overtime,
and that's your complaint...
Then it's quite possible that you have missed your calling!
Because God does not put on us, more than we can handle.

But, if you're putting in overtime because it's your passion
Then you just may have stumbled onto your reason for being.
That's if, by some measure, that this work that you do, pleases
God...

As for eating and playing, you can combine the two.
And enjoy the company of friends, family and loved ones,
Appreciating all that you have been given,
And maintaining moderation, as the Bible explains.

Rest.
But, if you are the over-compensator like myself,
And you feel like you still have not accomplished enough,
and work again you must...
You can work,
while you're resting,
Envisioning your success,
while you sleep.

FOOTSTEPS THAT WERE ORDERED BY GOD

If you stumble across one of God's lost souls,
help pick them up, and do what you can to help
put them back together again.
They're probably one of God's witnesses.
Just waiting to share with you their testimony.

It happened to me, it can happen to you.

I felt I was out in the world all alone,
without God's protection.
So, I started to look for love in all the wrong places.

But as we all know, God can reach us at any location.

One,
two,
three men...
before I knew it...
My life started to resemble that of Mary Magdalene's.

Who's that you ask?
Well they tell me:
She was dirty from the mistakes she made,
and, because of the mistakes she had made,
the people in town wanted to stone her,
but Jesus still loved her, and always treasured her company;
as he did all the other disciples, as well.

That's how I felt when God showed me my worth.

See, I can't tell you the whole story of the life of Mary Magdalene.
You'll just have to look it up,
or take my word,
that she was more than a four-letter word!

Well, now you can see,
why I can't tell the whole story
to you right now;
the pain is still fresh,
and I bleed at times,
from these memories left behind.

But, just like Mary Magdalene;
there was hope for her,
and there was hope for me.

No, it wasn't Jesus Christ, himself,
Who came for me;
to tell mankind not to cast the first stone...
but I saw a little bit of Jesus,
in this man's face,
from day one.

He took on great responsibility,
One that most men would never had,
or have run from.
Together, we raised three kids.
Never having children before of his own,
he began to provide a home.

Complete with a father,
something that every home should have.
He did what he could;
he did what a man should.
And what he couldn't do,
I prayed for the both of us.

Now after many years have passed,
it's time for me to pay my respect.
It's my turn to give back a little of what was given to me;
Some love and understanding.

And to this man without name I will say,
"No good deed goes unnoticed.
God knows what you have done,
Because your footsteps were ordered by Him;
I truly believe this!"

But now, what you must do is
take that same amount of loving and kindness,
and start applying it to yourself.
So that you will know just how much you are
Truly one of God's blessings.

IN THE NAME OF GOD, I PRAISE YOU

I know and call on Him,
the Man, Himself.
He helps me out,
When I can't seem to find my direction,
And I am stumbling along my path.

He gives me food for my soul.
He pays my rent.
When I can't seem to meet the minimum,
He does the maximum;
The miraculous!

He's my friend, my father;
My lawyer in the courtroom;
My teacher of life, and what I'm going through.
My advocate,
My voice, my employer;
He's my inspiration for writing these poems.

He's my rock, my shelter, my comforter.
He's the healer that has allowed me to never take sick.
He's my patience in the midst of this world.
He's the center of my joy, when I forget where I belong.
He's the owner of this heart, that bleeds for His people.
When they are in need and have fallen short,

He's the Man that has allowed me to see,
And tell the world, and not just show them:
"There is victory!
He's the Man Above!"

< 90 >

That keeps these hands praying,
In this day and age.

But, that's right I didn't tell you His name;
The name I call on, in my every situation,
That's God Above!

I know this is the part
where the world gets caught up,
Because everyone wants to claim Him.
Truth be told here,
He belongs to no one,
Because He belongs to everyone,
no matter the name;
Allah, Jehovah;
it really doesn't matter.

He's the God of all gods, King of all Kings.
The Supreme Being;
And let no man do Him under;
With words of destruction;
Blasphemy.

It does not matter to God,
Which name you have chosen for Him, in your life.
So long as He is God, all by Himself, in your life.

These are the blessings that He has given to me,
In my life, that had my own name on them.
And, this is who He is to me;
And, He who will continue blessing me,
So long as I know who's in charge.

Ask yourself:
Does the God that you serve do for you;

Any, or all,
Or more of the things,
That I have mentioned to you,
When you call on Him ?
By the name you know Him of?

If the answer is yes,
Then He's indeed in your life,
Who you say He is;
Both yours and mine
Do you think that's possible?

Go in peace,
And
God bless!

I WILL BLESS THE LORD, ALWAYS, FOR HE IS WORTHY

The feet were meant to carry our weight.
But our feet were also made to give praise unto the Lord;
And our hands the same.
That's why it feels so good when you're out at a club dancing...

You're using one of the blessings that God gave you.
But you're using this blessing,
That was meant to bring pleasure to the Lord.
To please yourself,
Not giving honor unto Him...

So then, why do people have a problem when you dance for the Lord, in church?

You are showing the Lord your form of worship, with your finishing touch!

Your mouth can sing or shout,
But your heart controls what your feet are feeling.
And none of this would be possible for us,
If we never were given the pair of eyes
that we have been given
To envision God.

It's a case of mind over matter;
The Lord does not mind if we sing our praises of joy unto Him.
Through all forms that he has given us.
So, what does it matter if you shout for joy,
And the person sitting next to you in the next pew over
Doesn't understand
Your song and/or your dance?
Thank Him, anyway,
According to the way you envision and accept Him.
You won't regret it!

< (94) >

PLAYING FOR THE WINNING TEAM

Ready,
set,
Go!

I'm ready to take off...

Ready to do the will of God,
And not the will of my own.

Ready to set a pace,
Ready to win a race,
Ready to score a touchdown
For the owner of the winning team!

Ready to share a story;
ready to hand out some glory.

Ready to teach, touch, laugh and cry.

Ready to look evil in the eye,
And hold my head up on high;
because at the end of this race,
I know I will finally see my owners face,
And, will have maintained the grace.

INVESTING IN MY OWN DREAM

I get it now, what I'm supposed to be:

I can see clearer now almost vividly...

Human beings must follow the rules,
and not work against them,
Giving themselves the opportunity
to reach full potential.

For it is when we are obedient,
And open ourselves up to this concept,
This is when we can see all that we were created to be.

A penny saved is a penny earned.
There is something to be said about a person who knows
The true meaning of the word obedient,
And works hard for what it is he desires,
Following through on his actions investing:
Sewing a personal oath into the lining of his own future.

GIVNING IT ALL UP

Lately, I've found myself giving it all up.
I'm worrying less about my outward appearance;
Focusing more on what it is that I do have to work with,
Letting it work for me.

What used to be my quick fix, healing agent, my solution
To any problem that existed;
My therapy and my favorite past-tune,
Is now a thing of the past.

My obsession that compelled me to shop daily
Has now come to a grinding halt.

I've traded in my sore feet,
Swollen ankles,
Anxiety attacks,
Headaches,
Those ridiculously long lines,
And empty pockets...
For something far greater,
And much more relaxing:
Time.
With myself.

I've been putting down those self-help books,
And picking up a pen,
And turning a few pages of my own.

I'm slowly drawing myself away...
From those relationships that gap the bridge
Between
Need
And
Want.
Turning to the ultimate,
Intimate relationship, which had been lost.

I've sworn off all the foods that have done damage to my body,
Over the course of the years.
I'm filling myself with soulful nourishment instead.

I'm talking less and learning more;
Enjoying life, the way it had been intended for me.

I'm tossing and turning less from sleeplessness;
Replacing the restlessness, with visions of peace, dancing over my
head. ·

I'm taking more time out for myself now,
And exercising moderation to avoid frustrations.

I've made a plan for myself and my life,
And prayed a prayer over it sending it on its way;
That by, and through, my faith.
I can and will.
Achieve-
All that is expected of me, from up above.

ONLY BLESSED

I'm not hungry anymore,

But I still get fed.

I'm not sad anymore,

But I'm still vulnerable,

And susceptible of being misled.

I'm not tired anymore,

But still require rest.

I'm not in pain anymore,

Because I only stand to gain.

I'm not rich.

I'm not poor.

I'm only blessed.

BEAUTIFUL DREAMER

Beautiful dreamer mind of my own:
Constantly turning, as the wheels of time continue to grind.

Beautiful dreamer mind of my own:
Takes me into a day and time, when there is war no more,
At my door.

Beautiful dreamer mind of my own:
Allows me to deal with life's harsh reality,
That one day there will be judgment,
And many will fall short.

Beautiful dreamer mind of my own:
Allows me to express freely the spirit
That dwells from within me.

Beautiful dreamer mind of my own:
Paints a beautiful vision in my head while sleeping at night,
And in the morning when I wake;
It allows me to recall these visions,
Through pen and paper,
Just as pieces to a puzzle;
Filling in all the blank space.

Beautiful dreamer mind of my own:
Whatever would I do without you,
In the driver's seat of all my creations,
And the Lord, My God, as my compass?

PUTTING IT ALL TOGETHER, TO MAKE A DIFFERENCE

Living peacefully, down deep within, there is another side of me:

One that lives peacefully, inside the walls of its existence.

One that manages to escape all of this world and all of its problems.

One that longs to do good, and that allows good to be done.

One that is full-in-Word and full of Word.

One that keeps no track of time, because she moves in God's speed.

One that can look inside the heart of a soul, and see exactly what that soul needs to function, and begins to work; feeding that soul chicken soup.

One that knows and sees too much for her own good, as well as the good of others.

One that holds the answers to many mysteries that will come to pass, and whom great responsibility has been given.

One that knows if and when her destiny should become fulfilled, radical change will also come to pass.

But, then there is the me that lives on the surface:

The one that on the real - struggles daily to maintain.

One that fights a demon, or two, of her own.

One that does not live so peacefully, and desires to follow the flow of the so-called "norm", and not always have to travel a route that flows against the "norm".

One that knows that no matter how hard she tries to become someone else, that God would only allow her to be who He has created her to become.

One that has no desire to hold a plate of responsibility over her head, or the desire to live to see change take place, but who also knows that this is not an option, that time is a wasting and that knows that with great responsibility, must come great effort.

Therefore, I continue with great effort to gather all of my flaws to meet all of my strengths, so that I can make my contribution in life count, and hopefully one day make a difference for myself and others.

< 102 >

MY PERSONAL BEST

When I first started, out I was a baby in Christ; not knowing what was expected of me, or what to expect. As time passed, I started to feel as if I was in the process of completing an obstacle course, and before the course was to be completed, that I would fall short.

Hurdles were carefully selected, for my own benefit, and then implemented into my path. They consisted of:

Change,
Attitude,
Love and
Personal Responsibility.

I was told that in order to please God as I so desired, that change, was not only called for; but that it was the inevitable if I were ever to complete this course that I was on. Then, it was told to me that once this set of changes had been made of myself, then further instructions would follow, with another list of

Changes:

Changes that would require fulfillment necessary...for one complete soul.

< 103 >

Then, each topic was revealed to me as the following:

Attitude:

That it should be dealt with, and if the time and place called for it, then I would know it and to be bold, in and through His word. That this display of attitude would be considered acceptable attitude, being on fire for God!

Love:

Although it was totally acceptable to verbally express to one another our love for one another, this would by no means displease or offend God, but through my actions should my deeds be weighed.
Personal responsibility:

To whom much is given much is required. That intimacy, if longed for over time will bring about spiritual maturity, and that I will achieve my personal best when and by the fruits that I'm bearing.

GOD IS THE FAIL-PROOF PLAN

I woke up this morning
Excited about the lesson
God showed me.

He told me that He's fail-proof
And to receive the victory
That all we have to do is except this.

So, I myself
Took it upon myself
To elaborate on this concept.

If God is fail-proof
Then, certainly, aren't we?
If everything we touched
Could turn to gold
Then, maybe, we ought
To start touching some things.

Maybe this is the reason why
We have been allowed to have
Loss in our lives.
Maybe some people
Start touching the wrong things.
Maybe this is why at some point
Some friendships die.

< 105 >

What would you touch in your life?
To have it turn to gold
Before your eyes?

For me, this question
Would be simple to answer.
But, for some,
I could see where
They might have to struggle,
In order to make the right choices.
I would touch the lives
Of as many as possible.

I would touch the lives of the old
By leading them to
The Only God I know, and serve,
To be by their side,
In their final hour.
"Yea, though I walk through
The valley of the shadow of death,
I will fear no evil."

I'd give the sick and infirmed;
Their so desired healing,
That it shall be by way of endurance,
And through long suffering,
That I shall lift you up.

I'd give the poor more
Than money could buy.
I'd give them back their riches
That have been stolen from them.
And, some of their riches
That have already been stored up for them .
Because, God has
An everlasting supply.

I'd give the hungry
Food for the soul,
And a cup to drink from,
That they may never have
To thirst again.

I'd give depression
The best medicine,
That a doctor could not define.
But, would have to consider
Faith is the substance of God's
Request, of Him asking us
To believe in Him.
When he seems out of season,
And when it seems we have no reason.

I'd give the abused and suffering
The answer to their question why?
Come unto me all who are weary
And heavily laden
For I will give you rest.

I'd give all the children
Grace and mercy,
Out of the mouths of the babes,
And the child shall lead the way.

I'd give the impatient
The wisdom to know
That they are acknowledged
And that this acknowledgment
Is confirmed by God.
I'd give them the ability to see the big picture
To look at, to help remind them
While they endure.

And, for all of God's soldiers
That are going to war since 2004,
And years to come:
Put on your whole suite of Armor,
So that the Devil
Has no chance
at winning the war!

HIS WISDOM, AND NOT MY OWN

I know on the road ahead of me, I know I have my work cut out for me.

Spending less time away from the frivolous things, which only carry a want and not a need.

Seeing myself, and others, in prosperity; doing the things that God asks of me.

Not taking the time out to pay attention to all the negative that possibly surrounds me;

Walking steadily into the battle, that will crown me glory at the end of my story

I will share and hopefully not be compared too...

But if my time comes and goes and no one knows...

God will know, because from me- He's allowed three lives to grow...

Thank you, God, for always having the wisdom for me when I had little to none to go on, and for helping me to know when to get things done!

< 109 >

COME, WALK WITH ME

Come walk with me, and let me show you the way to finding peace, in this day and age.

Come talk with me, and allow me to reveal a plan for your life that requires the signing of your name on the dotted line of a fail-proof plan.

One which entitles you to a lifetime guarantee of full- coverage of God's protection, and under His supervision;

For you will need Him, when you find yourself being hit with one of life's many collisions, or traps, that do exist.

Come walk with me, so that your footsteps, as well as mine, will be guided on our journey towards achievement.

Come walk with me and see peace, so that you can then go out and release it.

Come walk with me on my journey, and lend a hand, so that we may leave footprints in the sand.

Come walk with me, as we work together doing God's work.
Come travel on a voyage with me.

One which leads us on a path,
towards our passage back home to God, above.

THE HEAL THIER, THE WEAL THIER, THE WISER

Require nothing, but accomplish all.

Go in peace, but also seek it.

Do good, and allow good to be done.

Ask questions, but remember your teacher.

Prepare time for yourself, but also allow time to prepare itself for

you as well.

Give to others, and learn to accept.

Teach what you know; and when you don't know, hold your peace.

Live life as an example, but find grace in examples, made.

Hunger for nothing, but desire all.

Fulfill others, as you fulfill yourself, and you shall be

Healthier

Wealthier

Wiser

DID YOU RECEIVE IT?

Did you receive it, that day it was intended for you?

Did you find your blessing that God had air-mailed, special-delivery, straight to you?

Did you receive it, that "peace-be-still", in that hour of need?

Did you have faith in that footstep, when it led you to his door?

Did you receive it right on time, or was the time right that you receive it?

No matter the Day, Time, or Hour;

You receive it,

Keep it, and

Never let it go!

As He so desires us to be still, and know that He is God.

WHAT A FRIEND WE HAVE IN JESUS!

Who could ever know the beauty of it all, when beauty is seldom ever saw?

Who could ever know the pain you carry, when others are too busy recognizing their own?

Who could ever take the time out to care, when no one ever took the time out to care for them?

Who could ever rise above destruction, when it is constantly crossing their path and very little help is ever offered?

Who could ever know that they were marked for greatness, if no one ever told them so?

Who could defeat the undefeatable, if no one ever gave them the right suite of armor to prepare for the battle?

Who could ever change the history of mankind, if no one ever thought it worth fighting for?

Who could ever look at society without judgment, if they were never given the proper teaching?

Who could ever move from glory to glory, if they don't know the first thing about the topic?

Who could ever love the undesirable, if God had not first loved them?

Who could ever identify with this person, besides Jesus Christ, Himself?

WHAT THE ENEMY DOES NOT WANT YOU TO KNOW

We come in this world by faith,
And we don't leave this world,
Until having figured this out.
And it will be by the coming of our faith,
Its appointed job,
To carry us out.

But, if it were left up to the Devil,
Most of us would never figure this out.
And hardly any of us
Would ever accept its power,
Because he comes to steal, kill, and destroy
Our every movement, our every thought.

It is the enemy's job to create an illusion.
It is the enemy's job to try and confuse us.
But, it is God, Himself,
That would allow this to happen.
And why you ask, would He do such a thing?
To give us free will,
In hopes that we might call His name.

For some, I know,
This concept may seem hard to understand,
But given the chance
God always reveals His plan.

When given this life
It did not come with a set of instructions,
To tell us what to do,
When were in trouble.

But, for some
It resembles a roadmap,
Or even a puzzle,
That was not complete
With a set of instructions.

But God as my witness,
He knew some of us might think this way.
So, he planned ahead,
Creating the Bible
To be used as a tool,
To help us fulfill our every need.

THE THIEF

I didn't ask to come here.
I'm only a product of two people who thought that they could love;
But somehow that love took a turn for the worse and ended up all wrong.

No one took the time out to give me what I needed.
No one ever even asked me what it was that I needed;
Instead I was used to fill a void of an empty soul.

My joy and strength became personal belongings.
They were kept in his personal possession.

I didn't ask to shake hand with the Devil,
but he embraced me anyway.

This is the song of a soul that cried out for help,
and the song that only I could seem to hear.

This is also the owner of the same soul
That has found out that I am owed a debt:
To be Paid-In-Full,
In the name of Davida Coleman,
Which is worth seven times greater.
That, of which was stolen from my possession,
And, that I shall collect on!

THE SELF-FULFILLING PURCHASE AGREEMENT

Prophets and poets speak of a land, time, and of war
no more.
But this cannot happen until there is peace restored,
As the enemy draws closer.
Some of us are all too eager to welcome him into our homes,
and our hearts.
We greet him at the door with gifts such as righteousness,
strength and courage.

After a short time, an exchange of goods for services
makes this transaction complete.
Your bill has been rendered:
Paid in Full: One Complete Soul.
Now purchased, at low cost,
with no monthly financing fees...

And, as the clause would read on,
of course in fine print...
mandatory maintenance fees
for the up-keep...

So, there you have it,
the exchange is made,
you the self-fulfilling purchaser;
for the low cost of your:

Strength
Courage
Righteousness
And Soul

You are now the rightful owner of:

Fear
Doubt, and
Emotional Discomfort
...And, that's the good news...

The bad news is:

You will pay monthly maintenance fees,
which entails the following:

The self-fulfilling purchaser to give up a few more of his worldly
possessions, such as:

Dignity
Respect
Loyalty
Commitment
Honor
And Faith

In return for :
Deceit
Envy
Hatred
And Discontentment

So, shall this exchange and replacement take place until further notice.

So, there you have it, the moral to this short-lived self-fulfilling purchaser's story:
Be careful whom you welcome into your home.

Always remember:

The cost should not be countless.
As we have been paid for, in full, long ago;
by the blood of Jesus Christ.

< 120 >

SELF -DESTRUCTION

We all play a part in the enemy's eyes,
Self-demise,
Sit around and cry,
'Cause you don't even try...

Get high,
Your soul has to then pay a fine,
Turn around and stop,
And look shook,
Cause you stopped and took a good look
At your own self in the eye.

I sure do hope these words come back again,
Or, I'll remember them till the end.
Because after all,
Isn't the beginning the end?

THE DEVIL PLAYS A MEAN GAME OF FOOTBALL

The Devil plays a mean game of football
Hitting, tackling, and is most proficient at intercepting.
He sends his line backers to do his bidding,
Tackling us down when we are at our weakest.
And, if his team seems to be calling all the wrong plays,
Then he steps in himself,
Intercepting,
To guarantee a touch down
Ensuring his team the winning score.

At times in our lives,
When we feel like we have reached our lowest point,
And we have come to a crossroads,
And must make an important decision,
And after much contemplating,
You choose one choice, over the other,
And because of that decision you've made,
Something good happens to you?
And, you almost feel as if God has rewarded you for making the
correct decision?

Well I'm here to tell you,
Be careful of the gifts that you receive and accept, in your life.
Be sure that the package you receive has God's blessings written all over it.
It just may very well have been sent from the player himself on the opposing team.

And, if you feel like you know what I'm talking about...
And, that this has happened to you before...
You have not to worry, because God is the devil' s opponent, and not us...

And He comes fully-equipped, to handle the Devil's game
He's the full-back that scores the winning touch-down
For every one of his attacks, he attempts to throw at his people's way.

So, don't be a fool or be misled
By placing your bet on the loosing team,
God is awesome, and He can do anything!

< 123 >

HIS PLAN OF ATTACK

Visions of beauty don't always dance in my head.

Sometimes it's just the opposite instead.

Just as a mother reaches her arms out for her newborn child, he does just, that as he seeks me out.

He reaches out his unending arms, and tries to make appeal of himself to me.

At times, it's as if he is someone else with a face so tempting and appealing, at other times he is so revealing.

Satan, himself, playing a game catch-me-if-you-can.

This is how the struggle goes.

Two steps forward, and three steps back, is his plan of attack.

BECAUSE OF GOD'S GRACE, THE ENEMY HAS NO WEAPON

Torn, but not broken

Down, but not out for the count

Obedient, but resistant to submission

Tired, but not old enough that complaint should be made

Weary, but not unsure of His power

Weak, but strong

Hungry, but not eager enough

Leading, but seeking guidance

Pressured, but willing and able

Scattered, and put back together

Forgetting, but then remembering the duties that must be done

All this when the enemy is allowed in;

But only until God reminds me of grace,

Of grace,

Of grace.

FIERY FURNACE

It must be cold outside,
Because the furnace is sure turned up in here.
Realizing what God has asked of me.
I pray to God, I have the strength needed
To see it through.

I've been through the fire
Close to a thousand times.
So, now I must sit down,
And tell you
What I find to be true.

That it isn't the fire that makes you.
It's the fire that defines you.
And, once you're finished walking through it,
You come out on the other side;
Leaving all those bad character flaws
At the Devil' s door,
Where they belong.

The flames are
The polishing-up of us,
The adding on of the finishing touches.
For, our day that we stand before God,
To tell Him that we no longer feel the flames,
And we no longer claim the burns or scars;
The only thing that we claim is
God's love and mercy that He so graciously has extended,
To each and every one of us.

THE MESSENGER

I've never been an ordinary girl
Because of the visions I saw
I knew I could help people
Or hurt them really bad, early on.

I could help them with my eyes
And my mouth could speak the words.
I could hurt them by telling them what I saw.
Because people are always afraid of the truth,
Instead of just embracing it.

I ran from this major difference in my life
Because all I wanted to do is belong.
So, I made a few bad choices,
But God wouldn't allow this gift
To go wasted or lost.

Everywhere I turned
People needed something from me;
A mother, a friend, someone to listen to them
And, tell them where they went wrong.

Or they were just like me;
Needing some type of family
Where they could rest.

Somehow, by the grace of God
I was always able to do his bidding.
Even when I was surrounded
And in the midst of sin
I kept on going.

Now all I keep hearing is...
"There's work to be done.
There's work to be done."
But then I asked God,
"Do you know who I am?"
And He replied,
"Do you know who you are?"

"I came so that you may have life."
Were the words that were exchanged in my heart
For the line, "There's work to be done."

And, no, I don't think that I'm Jesus Christ, Himself,
But, just like God said, there's work to be done.
And miles to go before I can rest.
So, now by any means necessary
I must find the courage to pass this test,
And embrace what's waiting for me, at the end,
Because I am a Message.

I know this because, He told me so.
And, who am I to keep God waiting?
If He told me to go forth,
And bring, with me, His word?

KEEPIN' IN TOUCH WITH HIM

God wants me to keep the pen in my hand
To look at these words and bring them back again

God keeps this pen in my hand
To remind me of what it feels like to be in touch with the man

At times, it's as if I don't be written this stuff down,
Trying to capture every sound,
Every beat in my head, because that's what written is,
Feelin' your pen

But then again, it be a spiritual thing jumpin' off me

Glad that God took a hold of me keeps showin' me

Can't stop written these words down,
Until he says times up, you no longer owe me,
You've heard every beat, every word, every sound

I CAN'T BE REFUSED

I can't be refused because at the end of each day,
when you go to lay down.
And at the start of each day,
when you go to open your eyes,
I am the one that is there.
I am the one that opens those eyes,
and gives you not only a new day,
But, also, a new sight.
I am the one who shows up at your dinner table,
when you bless your meal.
I am the one you turned to for help,
when you were working real hard to meet ends meet.
I was the one to show up,
and meet your every need.
I am in the midst of everything you touch.
From the cup that you drink from,
that you shall never thirst again.
To the remote control,
that keeps you comfortable in your relaxation,
By exercising moderation.
I am in everything from the smallest, to the greatest,
To the latest, to the everlasting.
I am technology, biology, and psychology.
I am the ultimate, of all philosophy.
I am the hand that wipes away your tears,
when life begins to break you down.
I am time stopped, and turned over, again.
I can't be refused, because I am everything.
Now, and until the end.

< (130) >

CELEBRATION

Christinas, New Year's Eve, Hanukah;
You think you have cause to celebrate now,
Then just wait until He returns.
That's when we'll all rejoice together again,
Family all gathered around on the holidays
Isn't always the case for some.
Instead of celebrating that time of year,
They allow it to pass them by, wishing that it had never come.
The 4th of July, Independence Day,

But only for some.

Drive down the street, while the only influence,
That you're guilty of being under
Is the skin you're in...
And you just might experience the American Dream...

Remember Martin Luther King, he too had a dream...

So again, who's independence was it, that was really won?
When you have born and raised up the only thing that he can be
Is your black son?
To Veteran's Day?
Let's bring home the soldiers...
Only to lead them right back to wartime again...
To Mother's Day...
But wait a minute, don't we celebrate that every first day of the
month?
Well, the government does if the child's father can't:
To Father's Day...

131

Somewhere in May, or is it...?
I'm sorry, I can't seem to remember that one.

Just like so many fathers out here
Have forgotten they're the fathers of a child somewhere,
And that that child has needs, and needs them,
Now here's one for you to grasp!
December 25th, if we can't even get this day right.

Then how will all the others make any sense to us?
Half the world celebrating, spending the day in observance
Instead of recognizing...
While the other half are still stuck in the hows and whys...
Whatever the case may be, God would have you to know:
That Christ has died for us
And that rest assured, He's coming back for His people,
And that's when the real celebration will begin!

< 132 >

WALK BY FAITH, NOT BY SIGHT

It's so easy to forget
Who you are in this world
When there are so many things
We've created to distract us.

Colleges
To build the intellectual thought.
The Arts
To help us express ourselves.
The Media
To influence and filter our thought.
Books on every topic,
To distract your mind,
From His thoughts.

Any and everything to keep you
From knowing your own identity.

It's all too easy here,
Everything set up,
So that you will forget or never learn,
Everything set up to enable us,
Aiding in our own failure.

Life made too easy for some,
So they get comfortable,
And just start believing,
In what the world keeps telling them
Instead of going to God, directly.

But then others have it hard...
They start to believe
That they have to fight to stay alive,
The Devil might occupy these people's minds for a short time,
But The Lord Above is the owner of their thoughts, outright!

We all go through
This process of illusion, confusion...

To get back to where we started.
And the Devil knows this;
He knows that he's living
In and through us on borrowed time.

And it is not us
Who has to hurry up and finish this race,
Because anything that God gave us to do
He's also given us sufficient grace.
Although, what pace we choose to work off of
Is usually that of man.

Yes, the Devil has his hand
In many different areas of our life,
But it is the human being, in the end,
That allows him to have and take too much credit over them.

Yes, the Devil is a liar,
But at certain points in our life,
We're our own worst enemies.
And, it is at these lowest points in our lives that we find ourselves!

That we must walk by our faith, and not our sight!

< (134) >

GREATER IS HE, THAT IS IN HIM, THAN IS IN THE WORLD

Worry not little one...
For I will give you light when there is no sun.

The Devil has a pair of eyes, and, yes, he uses them to see...
But he's not greater than the power that be.

Despite what you have been told, he's not the enemy...
Only if you allow him, embrace him, letting him in.

I know because the Devil has come my way,
once or twice, to try and rape my soul...

But what he doesn't know, that I know:

Is that my soul has already been brought and sold,
well over a thousand years ago...

The next time you're feeling lost inside yourself,
just try to remember...

That no weapon forged against you shall prosper, and if God,
Himself, for you, surely then what man can be against you?

< 135 >

WHO'S WAITING FOR YOU?

If you're not ready to live
Then you're not ready to die

Because life begins
When we start to live
And doesn't end until it's our time

Our number is not called
By some random selection

But life is given to us without question

To become who we desire
If we have the heart

For some of us
We don't always have the start that we would have desired

But that's all irrelevant
Because it's not important were we start

It's how we finish that will count

I know for some
They think it's just the other way around

It's not how you finish it's how you start

But that's just the reason there still hanging around
Left to keep thinking

Until the rationalization hits them
That this life was theirs

But not for the keeping

The taking for one moment
Until they realize who's in control of it

The Beginning and the End

UNTIL HE COMES FOR ME

I will sit here in this room and write,
until there are no more words.

I will stay here, until the job is done.

I will write with this pen, until there is no more ink.

I will spread the word to those who can here;
and for those who don't have an ear, I will shed a tear.

I will express the Love of the Lord,
through my life and death,
until Jesus feels I am to be set free.

THE MESSAGE HE GAVE ME

If you can hear me,
Then I know you'll understand me,
I've come to bring you the Message at large.
That all you have to do is try and remember,
"Let Go, Let God!"

And at the end of this Message,
You'll know who's in charge.
He chose me to write the message down,
About the things I see,
So again, you could see the Message at large,
That the Man, Himself, remains in charge.

And, I know...take it easy,
Because this ain't easy;
For me to have to tell you
About the visions I walk through;
That one day,
We'll all have our chance
To meet the Man at large.

So, remember, go easy,
And just try to please Him.
Because...

One Day This Will All Be Over;
Ended.
And,
We Will All Have a Brand New Start.

A SINNER'S SONG

These words I share with you
Are like none other you've seen before,
Because many of you have witnessed the power,
But, just are either to embarrassed, ashamed, or confused,
To come forth and call out loud, the Lord's name.

For this reason,
I call on the Lord, to give me the strength,
To testify, and bear witness to what I have seen,
And hopefully in the process, along the way,
I will wipe my own slate clean.

This is not a sermon, from me to you.
It's a wakeup call, killing two birds with one stone.
In hopes that we both will receive our 911 call.
Because he's an on-time God.

Help is the message, He's crying out loud,
To save his people that won't fight for themselves.

This I pray to you, He would say,
"This is my world; learn to love me,
As much as you have learned to love my land,
That I have created for you.
And if you are one of those people who refuses to love my land,
Then you refuse both; My land and My hand."

God does not need help to put back together
What man has tom apart.
He's God, all by Himself.

But He seeks the witness out,
To remove all the doubt of the sinner's heart,
Who feels like they have a song,
And just needs a place to belong.

WAIT FORME

Wait for Me, when it appears that I am not around you.

Forget Me not, when it appears that I am the invisible.

Seek Me out, when you need an answer.

Know My name, when someone needs a kind word.

Allow Me to touch the soul of a man who cries a thousand tears, but is still able to speak My words clear.

Honor Me in the presence of thine enemies, and allow My heart to overflow into your hands, that they might receive a blessing through compassion you show.

Remember Me, always...

Never let Me go...

HEAVEN OR HELL: ONLY TIME WILL TELL

I didn't think it was possible for me to slip and fall down again.

I thought I had this thing called defeat licked, beaten; but just as I thought I had mastered trouble...

That's when I fell, only to have another lesson learned!

Seeming to have all the answers, and all the questions lined up evenly into a neat little bunch.

I found out that; Yes, I could possibly be serving myself...

What need do I have; what purpose can I serve?

Is it Myself, is it God, or is it His Love, from which I seek to serve?

With time it must pass, this need, this want if ever I am to make Heaven my home at last!

UNTIL THE DAY OF MY JUDGEMENT

Until my judgment day,
I will be like the fruit that bears knowledge;
ripening and waiting to be picked.

I will protect and guide the innocent from wrong,
and help build them until they are strong.

I will identify with some,
and others, I will pray amongst.

I will never look down,
but always look up.

I will remember my place,
but still live amongst my race,
keeping God's grace,
along the way.

I will
work,
work,
and work,
until my job
is done.

CROSSING OVER FROM PAIN: TO THE OTHER SIDE

Pain, pain, pain, all over again

Can't seem to shake it, because it's all around me

Not allowing me to set myself free

Can't climb under it, can't climb over it, can't go around it

All I can seem to do is walk through it

Can't understand why

All I can seem to do is try

Can't seem to make any sense of this place or even begin to figure out how a person could be led so a stray

Mistakes made, so easily, so readily; by my mindless thoughts of how my need met my want; silly of me, to even had to have such regret...

Anyway, too late for regret now, too late to play shut down

No time to crawl now, not even time to walk now, only time to run and fly time to play catch up, time to say good-bye...

Time to look evil in the eye, and laugh at its demise

Time to stay focused, and find out all the reasons why

Time to wake up in the future...

On the other side

BURNT OFFERINGS

I don't have much to offer You.

All I have is these words on paper, to touch Your heart;
Bringing life, from words deep within.

I don't offer You what is considered to be the leftovers in my life;
Instead I offer You just the opposite.

I offer You my burnt offerings of these words,
That daily I try to live by.

Just as you once, so long ago, showed me Your love and mercy.

Yes, Your love is more than plenty, more than sufficient;
For my cup runneth over.

For I may not have everything that I want,
But it is certainly clear to me that I already have
Everything that I'll ever need.

No, I have not made my fortune yet, but I know as I am told, that my
riches are already laid up in Heaven;

For, I treasure not the will of mankind,
but seek the kingdom of God instead.

And, that it shall be through faith and obedience;
That I will, one day, be laid to rest.

JOURNEY ON

What a life it has been, walking alongside Him!

What a journey I will travel, to complete my transformation!

What a difference a day can make, when you give from your soul!

What a year it will be, when I can truly see all that he has in store for me!

PASSING IT ALONG

Passing on the things that I have learned,
preparing for the changing of the guard.

Stepping aside,
as I watch a new guard.

Letting go, not holding on;
carefree, in understanding God's plan.

Passing on my words and thoughts to whom I love,
so that life won't seem so much of a mystery to them,
when my time has run out, and I'm no longer in existence.

These words will continue to bless.

GODSPEED

I don't want to lie down and wake up tomorrow,
knowing that I'm one step closer to my grave...

I don't want to grow old and die.
All I want to do is stay alive and try.

I don't want to set a pace that I will move along on to quickly,
and cause myself to miss out on enjoying my victory.

But, as my God would have it, I will move in His speed.

I don't want to leave this earth with unfinished business,
so I will stay in this race and continue on this journey,
until my last and final deed is...
Complete.

< 150 >

WHOSE REPORT WILL YOU BELIEVE?

It is by your own admission, that you will find your own truth
Whose report will you believe?
If they tell you that you have, not much time left to live?

Whose report will you believe?
If you cannot hear God's voice, clearly?
And you feel as if He no longer cares?

Whose report will you believe?
If they try to tell you that there are some sins that he cannot forgive
you for?

Whose report will you read from?
When they try to tell you that it is the end of the world and all that
exists?
And you are not yet quite sure how this will all end up?

Whose report will you believe?
When they try to tell you, that none of this makes any sense,
And is not relevant?
Because He never lived, and does not exist?

Will you believe in the report of the Lord?
When He tells you that He has a hand in everything that you touch,
breathe in, and that exists?

I came, so that you may have life...
Are you a believer of?

NEVER CAN SAY GOOD-BYE

I know at the end of this life,
I'm going somewhere.
So, what I have to do now is start to prepare.
Have to live my life as if each day were the last.
Making each day count for something,
And learning to seldom look back.
I have to rely on what I know,
And not be afraid of the facts.
Have to count up the cost,
Make some change,
Then give some back.

It is the human nature to believe what we are told,
But it's a completely different story when we are shown.
At the end of each day,
We have our free will that has been given to us,
To face the next day and what is to come.

But, death is the only area
Where most of us are left to guess,
To learn something of our own,
To learn some things that are ours;
And only;
our own.

It's a time to make our last entry
Into the book of our lives.
It's the writing of our last chapter,
And about saying our good-byes.
It's the last chapter of our lives,
Where our soul is carried back to the light.

THE LORD GIVETH,
AND THE LORD TAKETH AWAY

I don't bring life, and I am certainly not the giver of it...

But, I am aloud to live and enjoy it.

To what capacity, that decision is left up to me!

Today, I realized this as I watched a human life slip away;
and a soul journey home, to its final resting place.

"The Lord giveth, and the Lord taketh away."

I am fortunate to be counted amongst the living,
and having been blessed with this knowledge,
this day.

AND, IN THE END,
I WILL BRING YOU JOY!

Joy comes in the morning ...
Now where have I heard that before?
And how many times?
How do you find joy?
In the midst of disparity floating all around you?

Mothers growing up motherless;
Raising up another generation of whose child is that?
Fathers walking away from what is supposed to be their joy;
And in some circumstances, doubting that that child was ever even their baby boy.
So, they do what they know from seeing?
And, what they will later on at some point in their life?
Learn that it is was wrong to deny their first born?

Walking, running, never even looking back; to claim their child, or give them a last name...
Now there's a thing called a paternity test...

Who would have ever thought that something that God created, that was supposed to be sacred, could get so messed up?
But then again, we are human beings and Murphy's Law of Relativity is that:
"Whatever can go wrong, will" go wrong.
Who would have ever known that a father would, could or should ever question his own?
But don't blame the Man Above...
He knew it could, would and never should have happened.

So He planned ahead for the day, and wrote down a set of
instructions.
And, don't blame Him either, if you never bothered to read them;
The instructions are there and clear, and he won't force you to read
them.
But He strongly suggests it.
Besides harming, no arming yourself with the truth, what will it hurt?
Even when you purchase a vehicle it comes equipped with two
things?

The owner's manual and the guarantee.

And, as for us, we own neither.
He owns the vehicle that you call your life,
And yes He has guaranteed you a fruitful one,
So then, when will you receive the joy you desire?
The minute that you pick up the owner's manual and read through it
twice...

Read your Bible, it's your comfort in YES, this day and age...
And remember, He felt our pain long before we ever experienced it.

Read about it!

< 155 >

FINAL VICTORY

If this is all there is, and this is all I am, then this must be my final victory! But if there is more too me than what meets the human eye, then the question still stands; who really am I?

I believe in what I see, and what I see I believe in, so now the question is put before you, does this make of me a bad influence? I believe that through hard work, I can achieve my ultimate goal. I believe that a strong will shall carry me through the toughest of moments in life, and that opportunity seized makes a wealthier individual.

Yes, I believe in a higher power, but what is it that people mean, when they say they have a personal relationship with this power that be? If we are all created equal, then isn't our connection to this higher power equivalent too, not greater than or less than? I don't feel as though I am in any danger of losing what I have worked hard for, because I continue to work hard for the upkeep. I don't feel as though I am a threat to anyone else and least of all, certainly not to myself! I live my life in the here and now and I don't see what the problem is, in fact who even said there is a problem at all? I don't know who would agree or disagree to my type of existence, if any at all, all I can say is for this lifetime in the here and now I am content.

"Then the lord spoke to the man who was filled with such content in his heart saying unto him; the steps of a good man are ordered by me!" (Psalm: 37-23)

"Are you he who lays up treasure for himself and is not rich toward me?" (Psalm: 12-21)

"Therefore I say to you; do not worry about your life, what you will eat nor about the body, or what you will put on. Life is more than food, and the body is more than clothing." (Luke: 12-22, 23)

"But seek the kingdom of God, and all these things shall be added to you." (Luke: 12-31)

"For What Will It Profit A Man If He Gains the whole world, and Loses his own soul"! (Mark: 8-36).

Then as the Lord began to turn and walk away as He would leave the content man with this last parable:

"I am Alpha and Omega; the Beginning and the End. Who is, and who was, and who is to come, the Almighty". (Revelation 1-8)

"I am your Final Victory!"

COMPLETION

Death is not our formal goodbye, or the end to our dwelling, as we know our existence to be.

It is not about our Last will and Testament.

It's not about dying and leaving something behind

It's not about leaving a lasting impression, on those of whom, those which we love,

It's not about living on borrowed time,
and trying to defeat the inevitable.

But what it is about...
is the coming to terms with the unavoidable.

It's about the finishing up of the unfinished.

It's about the completing of the assignment that you have been handcrafted
for.

It's merely plain and simple; our soul, crossing over to the other side,
to reach a place that some already know about, and call their home.

< 158 >

And, if you can accept this fact, then half the work is already done. You've already begun to reach your destiny, but the journey is not over yet. There's more for you to know.

All that's left now is, for you to realize that you are strong enough to reach:

Completion of this one last task: to make Heaven your Home, at last.

ENTERING INTO THE THOUGHT OF ETERNITY

I know I've entered into a place now, that I know I'll never leave again.
Because I have found the reason for my existence.
And, although I am not dead yet, I feel like heaven is right here on Earth.
And the reason why I'm so happy is...
Because I feel closer to God.

I've found out that you don't have to die
Before you can have the ultimate relationship with God.
That He is with you wherever you are,
And although you can't see Him,
His ability to reach us here on Earth
Is the same here on Earth, as it will be when we're in Heaven;
And we have crossed over to the other side.

He will be with us, and reach us no matter where we are.
So, we can receive not only his blessings,
But also that personal one on one relationship with him that we so desire.
So that we can remember not to quit.

He would then remind me; that this is why we live.
He is the reason we live!
Now, I no longer carry with me the impatience to know what's waiting for me on the other side.

MY CHARACTER: MY CONTENT

Who would I possibly be, if I wasn't me?

I'd possibly be the one to change history,
somebody to restore a couple of things.

Somebody who would touch the world and embrace it,
not just another fool trying to erase it.

I don't know if I'd do it by picking up a pen,
don't know if I'd even be able to blend.

All I know is I'd see things through to the end...

I wouldn't change the content of my character,
no matter what people said...

or thought...

I would know who was in control of my thoughts.

WHAT KIND OF MARK
WILL WE LEAVE?
HE WILL DECIDE!

People in this world, want, desire and try so hard to leave their mark.
And during the course of their attempt,
They fail to realize what they have been given.

That it is not their duty or their place to decide whether or not
If it has been willed to them, to leave their mark on the human race.
But, it is that, the job of God- and God alone,
Who will do the deciding.
That is why many men die broken hearted.
Failing to realize that they were the exact mark that God
would have wanted.
So long as their life resembled Him.

And the things that they had been given
Were gifts from God, and part of their mark.

If you believe in what I have told you,
Then you will know that you won't have to feel compelled,
To climb a mountain, it's already been done.
You won't have to pay a cost, you've already been brought,
You won't have to over extend yourself;
Because God will be there in the end.
You don't have to do anything extraordinary,
But you may feel as if you have been asked to go against all odds,
But all you really have been asked to do is; wait on, and accept the
Lord.

< 162 >

JUST A TEST

How can I teach you anything
when you seem to know everything,
yet you still know nothing? Not being able to move past
your own Ignorance
because you're stuck,
trapped inside your own existence.

Never taking time out to come out of your own self
long enough to see, and recognize,
that there's a whole world out there.
Selfish and greedy, I have my needs.
My car, my house...
Oh that's right,
they tell me life don't really revolve around me,
no matter how hard I work to take care of my responsibilities.
As long as I'm paying my bills on time minding mine,
why the hell should I have to give a damn about society?

After all, who cared for me when I was just a boy?

Who was there for me, when I wanted my first car?
needed that leather? had to pull it all together? and be a man?
Oh that's right...

In your eyes, I don't cry,
cause I'm still stuck inside.
After all, who are you to judge me,
isn't it said that I'm not done,
till He's finished with me?

Who was there, when I cried all alone,
became a man, raised a family, made mistakes,
to get back up and stay in the game?
Who was there with me or better yet who even cared?

God was there don't be so surprised!

He felt your pain and believe me, He cried;
but to use your words...He's not done,
He's not finished yet,
hang in there this is all just a test!

< (164) >

THE PARABLE OF GOD'S UNTOUCHABLE(S)

Let me sit down to tell you this one. Three men came for me in the middle of the night, put me in a car, and took me on what was to be my last ride, and I was made to do the driving. One sat in the front seat up close next to me; the other man sat in the back seat. He was the one giving all the orders, and taking charge of what he had marked for my end. He told me to drive to the local dump, and as we pulled up, he told me to drive down half way through, and shut the car off... when I picked the spot. I shut the car off, and the one in the back seat jumped out, he told the man in the front seat to "do his job".

Up until this point, I wasn't sure who sent them. But, when he told the other man to "do his job", I figured it out. As he closed the car door behind him, that's when it began. I had to save myself. I didn't know how, but I knew I had to try. I began to look around...checking the car out...

"I have no weapon!", I thought, as I looked at the guy; trying not to make him feel as if he were the one who was being threatened.

Then, at that point, I heard God speak:

"Davida do what you do best: speak."

So, without question, I began to speak. I told the man I knew that he really didn't want to hurt me. He said, "Lady you're crazy; you don't even know me."

I told the man that I knew something better than him, and that was his heart. Because despite where I was at, and despite what it looked like, this man was a good Inan; fighting for his own life. He'd just been down on his luck for a while, and needed a job. And, before the night would be over, he would be given a second chance, at a new start.

God allowed me to see past my own circumstances at that point, to do what might have been my last job for Him, so I began to speak, again.

I told him that I didn't think he fully understood what he was doing. And, if they were caught, that the other two men would fully blame him, saying it was his idea. When I told him this, he looked at me and asked, "Who cares?"

So then I knew I had to tell him what I really saw. I told him that, in less than an hour, I would be shot. That help would come and find me. And when they did, I would still be living and well enough to tell them what happened, despite whatever attempts they would make, to try and take my life. I asked him then, was that what he wanted? He looked at me, and it's as if God had frozen his hand in that position it was in. Because, the whole time I was doing all of this talking, I had a gun to my head. So he told me then, to just drive off.

Before I could move my foot towards the pedal, he had changed his mind, he told me to stop. That just because he couldn't go through with it, didn't mean I wasn't dead. He said that his friend would come back and "do the job". He said that he had a family, I think of four, and that all he wanted was to take care of them. I asked him how killing me would take care of them? I guess that's when he knew, that he could not do what he was sent to do.

< 166 >

He told me that the man that hired them paid a great price, and that he would not rest until I was dead. I wanted to ask him about who sent him, but I already knew. But before I could ask the question, he had already described him to me. He said that all that he could remember about him was this blue suit. I found that ironic, someone · paying you a pretty penny to end a life, and all you can remember is a blue suit?

But then again, it didn't surprise me, because that's how the Devil makes his entries into our lives. He comes on strong; to get us to do what he wants us to do, then disappears without a trace, leaving you to figure out and clean up the mess that he has made.

Well, at this point the second guy comes back, and jumps in the front seat too, yelling at the first about... (why hasn't he killed me yet and...?), what is all the chit chat about?

That's when he ordered the first guy out of the car, so he could finish the job that was started. The guy jumped out of the car and gave me a look, as if it were nothing else he could do. I was told to start the car and move down a few spaces, to where this abandoned bus was parked, blocking the view, of where we now were at. I knew that there was no reasoning with this man, because just like the first, I had seen his heart. And inside the heart of this man was nothing, but stone, and I told him so. I began to speak one last time, or what he would have it to be, so he thought.

< 167 >

I told him that it made no sense in me fighting for a chance with him, because at some point in his life, his heart turned cold, and had stopped beating. He laughed and agreed with me. He said he was not like the other punk. He asked me if I believed in God, and I told him, "No, I know Him." He laughed again, and said well get ready to go to Him. He said on the count of three, we'll do it together, so he counted to three, with the gun pointing at my chest. So I clinched my fist and began to chant: "God keep me safe, you are my rock and my strength, God keep me safe."

And before it was over, I was shot three times. Once in chest, a second time in the stomach, and a third hit, which had traveled downward.

As the first bullet went in, I barely seemed to feel it. So I then began to pray again, but quietly: "God keep me safe, you are my rock and my strength, to see this thing through".

At that point, I tried to open my eyes, but something told me to keep quiet, and to keep them closed, and that's when I heard the door close, and the footsteps disappear...

I still laid there quietly, not talking out loud anymore; but talking to myself. I heard God say to me, that I did have what it takes, to pull myself through.

That's when I heard a set of footsteps walking back towards the car. I heard God speak to me again at this point. He told me to lie perfectly still, because we were going to trick him, make him think I was dead. I could hear the voice say just to make sure, so that he could receive his pay. That's when the third bullet hit me, and although I felt it hit me, I don't know where I was hit, because I was starting to turn cold. As soon as the bullet hit me, I felt him check for my pulse and say, "Good, she's dead." He walked away, for the last time, leaving me to bleed; and thinking I was dead.

But God's voice stayed with me the entire time, telling me what to do. He told me to open my eyes, and call for help, and by doing this someone would hear my cry and come to help. I tried to speak, but it was as if my voice was gone. I managed to let out some type of sound that managed to get through; and at that point, that's when God told me that I would pull through.

Just as God said, not even five minutes had seemed to pass, since I mumbled that sound, as a rescue truck appeared and before I knew it, they were going to work.

Again three men would jump out, as the first approached the car, and tried to take a good look at me. The first man was shocked, by what my appearance seemed to be. He turned back around and headed for the truck, and told the other two guy's, "Naw, man, I can't do it. That girl's really messed up". So, the second one walks over and gives me a look, and he too, is shook. But he looks at me, and manages to put on a fake smile, and begins to tell me that I'm all right.

I'm fully conscious at this point, and begin to speak, while still clinching my fist with one hand, and the other free. I begin to tell the medic how to save my life. I give him orders on what I needed. Some gauze and some bandages, to stop the bleeding, and radio ahead, but those were the paramedic's words, as I listened in, as he began to tell his friend, that he had never seen anything like this. He returned to me, and said that he must be honest with me: that there was a good chance that I may not pull through, that I might die, when they begin to lift me up, onto the stretcher.

< (169) >

With the hand that was free, I reached for his hand, and I told him, that I knew I would live. I told him that my life was not in his hands, and that I know it probably felt that way to him. But it just so happened, that his hands were the pair that God chose, because He knew that he could use them to work through. He looked at me, and I believe he saw God, because the reply he gave, was that of a smile that could light up the sky.

"Lady on the count of three will do this together", were the words I heard again. "One, two, three!", I'm lifted and onto the stretcher.

Off to the hospital, that was ironically known as Mercy Hospital, and believe it or not, the medic actually thanked me, saying "Lady we've done all we can."

He rushed me through the doors, with his assistants, and began to tell the doctor-on-call the status of my condition. I look up from the stretcher; and tell the doctor I can move my right hand, but my left one is numb, and that I was numb, from the waist down.

The doctor looks down at me and says, "You are a miracle! How did you survive, to make it here this far?" I looked at the doctor and said, "With the help of God."

I told him not to worry, that God had told me that I would not die.

He told me the chances of anyone ever surviving what I had been through, and he said that he now knew that God does exist.

FOR THE LOVE OF JESUS CHRIST

If a human life is worth living
Then certainly it is worth protecting.

But the question
You must ask yourself here is,
Who's in control?
Who really cares?

Homeless sleeping on benches,
Or wherever else a place can be found?
In the dead middle of winter?
While the rich and middle class
Keep walking in circles all around them,
As if they were transparent of sight.

Love,
Peace,
Hope, and
Prosperity:
Isn't that we all seek to find?

But the human condition can be cold,
Great minds do think alike.

The poor and misfortunate,
That have very little to give,
Are willing to lay down their lives for them.

And those who are able to give,
Not only give such little thought to this process,
Barely thinking twice.
That this could be their reason for living,
And that their job is similar to that of Jesus Christ.

Who will prosper then?
If they are left alone to die?
And never given a chance?

Who will hope they find peace?
In the midst of this world, and how it exists?

Who will have the Love for them,
As the Love of Jesus Christ?

GOD DOESN'T DO JUNK

I'm not Maya Angelou, Benjamin Banneker or W.E.B Dubious.

I am only one voice, speaking clearly about the visions I'm blessed
with, as if I ever really had a choice.
I didn't choose writing, God chose me, to write down some of His
own beats, according to what I have seen.
He speaks to me everywhere I go, all day long, telling me to write it
down, write it down, so they'll know and understand.
As if it hasn't already been written down before, and as if it hasn't
already been said.
But who am I to argue with God, if He says so?

He speaks to me about the areas of our lives that cause Him great
concern, so here goes:

Money:

He feels as if we can never get enough. And asks the question; how
much will be enough? And whom by man's merit and standard of
judgment, should he will it to, if it were left up to you to decide?
Whose hands on this earth right now, if given it, are worthy of it? Is
it you? Who's to be first in line to receive, and who should be last?
And who could handle all the responsibilities that would come along
with it? If He did give you the total amount that you wished to have;
then he asks, would this define your love for Him? Or, confirm His
for you? He reminds us that on every dollar bill, we are told that it is
in God, whom we trust. So then, if we trust in Him so much, then He
would ask- don't you love and trust in Him enough to know that
your riches are already laid up? That the first shall be the last, and

< 173 >

the last shall be the first. And the Lord giveth, and the Lord taketh away.

Churches:

Many churches are half-empty, yet every day another is setting up. And God would have you to know that, under One Nation of God, is He coming back! And to the non-church member, He would have you know, stop judging his Christians, as He is God, all by himself.

This area is His job, and His alone; that He will see fit to do with. Stop making every kind of excuse that He's already heard, the biggest one ("I've gotta get clean first"), because that will not stop Him from doing His job of judging all of us.

Christians:

Christ-like people, He would have you know that we are His chain; connecting the links. Where there is the strongest link, so lies His strength, and so where there is the weakest link, we all stand to tumble and fall. This is one of the reasons why the non-church member decides not to join and become a part, which brings me to religion, and the study of God.

< 174 >

Religion:

God is not work, He just is. He does not go by any labels that man creates for Him. He only operates off of them because that's what we need Him to do. As He has told you before, He would never leave nor forsake you. I could go on with more, and probably should, but for now I'll leave you with this thought:

If you would like to know, and speak to, God in this capacity...

All you have to do is start to remove the junk.

Because junk is: the things (issues) we allow in our lives, to keep Him from ever having conversation with us. It's what keeps God distant from us, and doing His part.

Remember this: God does not do junk...we do!

< 175 >

THE UPPER ROOM

For quite some time now, I've had a vision of a place called The Upper Room. The Upper Room first appeared to me, while asleep. The Room was filled with colors so bright, but there was only one light that stood alone and shined ever so brightly; but before I could reach that light I would first walk through a bed of flowers that carried every kind of scent. There were Tulips, Orchids, Roses and Daffodils that would meet my feet to greet my presence, and at the end of the long bed of flowers was placed a door.

To enter this door did not require that I hold a magic key, nor did it require of me to quote some special password; the only thing that was required of me in life, was that I Acknowledge Jesus Christ, and accept Him as my Savior; to be escorted into this Upper Room, called Eternity.

So, upon my arriving at this door, I spoke the only words that I could think of that opened the door:

"Father I stand here before you humble as your servant, meek of life, but bold in your cause. Let my life and deed show in the Book of Life, for it has already been written. Let my record show that I give all honor, glory and praise unto Your name only."

This is when I was allowed passage in.

Once inside, many people, from every direction, gathered around me, giving me special attention; but dare I ask the question, "What did I do to receive such a warm welcome?"

Before this thought had a chance to leave my mind, I was given the answer to that question I had wanted to ask:

A scroll was placed in my hand that would read as follows:

"For a lifetime of service rendered, in the Name of our Father and Jesus Christ. All present this day honor your presence, and request your presence to feast with us, at this time."

Then, I heard a voice say, "Come, walk with me where the streets are paved in gold, and the street lamps are always lit. Let us rejoice this day for she has returned home to us."

And, as the vision had clearly appeared to me, so did it quickly vanish. When I opened my eyes, all had been revealed to me; all of what I must do.

I must always honor and praise God, by putting Him first. Because "God so loved the world, that He gave He only begotten son."

REDEMPTION

Whatever I build up here,
it will be matched on the other side.
And my love for God,
that I have for Him, with me now,
Will be equivalent too,
on the other side.

When I stand before Him,
at the moment I die,
So if I don't get it right now,
I can't expect to reach the other side.
So all of us should know this now,
and this should give us reason to really try.

I grew up feeling that the world
wasn't really for me.
Because of the miracles that God always showed me,
I couldn't tell many.
At times I couldn't tell any,
I could only tell the people that He would allow me,
But I didn't get angry,
until I knew what I had.
And then I wanted to tell all,
but God kept me planted firm on His word.
And told me when the time was right,
then I could tell the whole world.
Now this time is here,
and there's no time for me to be scared...

Because this is bigger than me,
My needs,
My family.

The world is in need of repair
I asked God why now,
why not then,
why not yesterday,
why not tomorrow?

But the answer was simple to me, before He could answer.

I thought, because tomorrow may be too late...
But that was only my guess, God would then answer:
My people are living in poverty...and of the worst kind:
Mentally.
They lack the concept that much has been given.

So that all, and not just many, would gain.
He speaks of the killing of every kind,
and he does not leave out the soldiers at war.
He feels their pain, saying that
the ones dying in Iraq are not dying in vain.
"Redemption" is the word that I heard him speak clearly...
If I were to keep my mouth shut now,
many people would go without a healing.

He would advise, that we must know that we cannot fix it all.
Definitely, by all means keep trying,
but to bring our troubles and concerns by him first,
because that's His job!

The Starving and Hungry:
He says that if His Son knew the answer to this question,
when he sent him for us, and showed us the way,
why are we still hungry, today?
Try, try, try again. That he won't spell it out for us.
But, to check out selfishness and greed,
That they've been around since the beginning of time.
And, that He will not stand for it.

"Again, Redemption, Davida:
this is not the time or the place to save just your own soul...
I Love you all, and I do not look for redemption, I expect it!"

Those were the words I heard.

< 180 >

A TIME AND PLACE, FOR EVERYTHING

Always live each day, as if it were your last:

Make each moment count as if it were your last breath you are about to take. But if you should mess up and make a mistake it's OK, because we're only humans and God created us this way. Find your purpose and make it happen.

Become eager and have a great passion at and about what it is that you do...

Remember that God has chosen and appointed you to whatever this task is that He has chosen for you, and it is you and only you, that he had in mind when he designed this task that he hand crafted for you.

Be open and honest, when you deal with others.

Put no faith in man as at times you will find that they will let you down, even hurt you, but remember there's such a thing called prayer; something that will always be around if no one else can't be near, tell it to God, and He can make it all disappear.

Always keep your faith with you, wherever you go!

Try not to let it run on low. Remember, just as a car requires its fuel, the body and spirit require similar food. We do this, by praying and going to church, but most importantly by starting each and every one of our days by opening up our eyes and talking to God, putting Him first.

If, for some reason this all becomes a bit too much for you to handle, remember that you do have the answer to the problem. The solution to your problem is down deep inside you; you just haven't brought it yet to the light. Remember that the substance of faith can be built upon while you're working your issues through. And, if you still find yourself experiencing some difficulties after reading this through, and feel as if you have nothing else to go on, you have a mouth. So open it up, lift up your hands and pray, pray, pray and God will command all the ugly away!

Know that you were born to be a blessing!
Know that you were born to be His blessing, so do just that.
Become a blessing; help others just as He has helped you.

Be aware of your time, and put it to good use!

Time is such a small word in our English language that has been assigned such a great task in each of our lives, but seldom given much thought. It was around before us, it is with us, as we grow, and will continue to exist, when we are no longer in existence.

Time can even reveal a little bit of our own identity, if we allow it. My advice to you on this topic would be this; to try spending more of your time doing things that are required of you that are not of man, but of God, and less time fulfilling yourself.

For this generation, coming up: remember that it is vital that you exercise the use of the word moderation into your daily diet, so that you will have enough energy to complete your task that we talked about earlier. Do give some thought to this word and how it will affect you and your life, and what role you will play in its definition in your life. As you move along life and grow, think about what type of person do you see yourself becoming and what this word does for you? Better yet, what you do for it? Ask yourself what kind of mark do you wish to leave on this life you have been given?

Try and make an effort to be punctual, because after all no one wants to be late to his, or her, own funeral.

Always turn brass into gold...

By following these life examples that you have been told, you're sure to become a success...

God Bless!

< 183 >

THESE ARE MY WORDS

This is life passing you by, in a blinking of an eye.

If you don't want to tell it to someone else, tell it to yourself.

Put it on paper, because paper doesn't have a mouth.

I write, because these are my words.

My words speak, for themselves.

They are only my thoughts, put to paper, from pen.

To capture this moment, that I'll never see again.

We often take for granted our...everything.

Our time, thoughts, words and moments...

So, I write them down, so at some point in time,

I can recapture them.

7 DAYS: DAY ONE

Be patient, as you wait for Me. Learn to find peace, even in the midst of endurance, and when you have come to the point when you have reached this place (then and only then) you will be a valued commodity.

You will become subject to change, but your path you travel will be less likely to unravel. You will worry less, sleep more and offer yourself, as only you have to give.

You will be frequented less about the troubles that others may appear to have. Because, you will know that just as I have created a masterpiece of a plan so great for you, and your life, so shall I do for all those, who appear to be heavy-laden with troubles of the world.

Take this time now, to stop and recognize all that you are, all that you are worth, and all that you shall become. Over the next seven days, journey through your past and present; pick up the tools along the way, which will help you build your successful tomorrow.

And, while you're on your journey, Davida, leave no stone unturned.

7 DAYS:
DAY TWO

Tears fall from my eyes when I think of all the mercy and grace God has shown, and given to me. The first day I was given this task, I didn't know what God was up to, or what He expected of me. But with sound mind, I would put the question before God, of what words would I put to this paper?

Would this paper, somehow, turn out one day to be the answer to a question, elsewhere down the road? Or was it part of a process of me merely coming to terms with my God, on the level He would have me on with Him, for that moment, day or week? Or was this God's way of reaching out for my attention, as my attention had seldom been focused on him in the past week; due to my flesh, and the weakening state of it.

As I was apparently falling quickly through the cracks of an emotional conflict with myself, and had begun to start to doubt my abilities, capabilities, and all of my existence. I began to experience feelings of having been put too, or through, some type of test. And the verdict on my Christianity would either reap or sow, from the words that I would put to this paper.

That is when God spoke to me and the words were loud and clear:

"Peace! The best is yet to come!"

I was to find peace, in and through my own word, that I so willingly lend out to others, to comfort them. I was to trust in myself, as well as in Him!

I now had to administer a little of my own healing agent, towards my own direction. The Message I received this day was:

To speak the word affluently, intellectually, clearly and Godly (meaning with love).

The Message would be received in, and through, peace:
Because that is what God so desires all of us;

To seek,
obtain, and
to maintain.

"Peace.
Be still."

< 187 >

7 DAYS:
DAY THREE

I found myself asking the question; who am I to think I can speak?

What qualifications do I bring to those whom I speak? With this one question alone, do I stay still and silent, awaiting the all-clear, or do I speak about what's inside of me? Do I speak about the truth as it has been revealed to me, or do I wait until I have obtained the proper education or training, that would qualify myself to stand up and speak? Or do I continue to do what it is that I seem to do best? Do I continue steadily down the only path that I've ever known, and that is to stop and aide, lend a hand, speak a kind word and pray for or with those in need? Or do I put this completely on hold, and reach out to fulfill a dream of my own? Do I obtain a degree in a specific area killing two birds with one stone, sort of speak; bringing some self-gratification to myself and receiving the expertise at the same time to complete the task?

At this point, God would then deal with the question and me at hand, giving me scripture as guide. He pointed out to me; that if it were not for the mistakes I have made in life, then experience wouldn't have been such a good teacher. And that the compassion that I speak to others with, would not come from the depths of my soul, and that without and if not for my checkered past. I could not have touched so many lives. And, that yes he could have chosen anyone else to do his will, but it was me who he has chosen to move the un-movable from in, and around myself.

God had been speaking to me the last few weeks on the word, the importance of knowing the word, and when to speak the word, and this scripture came to mind. Be quick to listen, slow to speak and slow to wrath.

God's message today for myself was to, yes know the word, but also remember that there are some who are called to the word and some who are appointed. And that each of us must know our own calling. The word is within me because He has instilled it, and that I should get behind Him, follow Him, and He will lead me to whom to listen. Once there, to be accurate in my speech, and to never judge while

there. No I could never be God, or replace him. But if God is opening a new door up for me to entire into, and if I am called-sayeth the Lord, then who am I not to open the door and entire in?

< 189 >

7 DAYS:
DAY FOUR

Today, I prayed to God about an answer to a question I had on religion. It was about the Muslim faith. I asked God about His people, and of their following of their faith, pertaining to Him?

After the question was asked, I then prayed again over this Muslim newspaper that had been left with one of my two sons who had recently paid a visit to a Muslim Mosque.

As I sat on my son's bed, I began to pray for him: Lord keep my son on high, protect him and shield him. If this is the enemy who has come and has tried to find an entrance into this house, then let him seek and find nothing. And if it is the work of you Lord who wishes to speak through example, then surely send a word along with this lamp if it must shine on my son, if he must see this light.

Then, I was finished and all there was left to do was to wait. In church that Sunday, a guest speaker would stand and speak to the church of a man who had once given his life to Buddha. Before finding his way back home to God.

When God speaks to all, He will always speak both clear and loud enough, for his audience. If you tend to have somewhat of a doubting nature, then he will always send roadside assistance, sort of speak.

< 190 >

In Christianity, we call it confirmation; that yes (I'm speaking to you directly type of message).

In day four's message, God's answer to my question went something like this, "I am Alpha and Omega, I am the beginning and the end. I have come so that you may have life. I am not a way of life or a lifestyle. I am life! I am not Catholic or Protestant, nor Pentecostal or Baptist."

I am life, and all that is in its existence, abundance, fullness, and completion. These are the names that are acceptable, and truthful. As I am the Way, the Truth, and the Light. All these words are representation of myself. You ask, are these my people? Then, you will know if what they say is the truth:

Let no man be afraid to stand alone;
To tell my story,
And, let light be, therefore, their glory.
So if they come before you and speak, this shall all come to pass, as it will all be revealed:

"I belong to no one group, organization, symbol, or people...
Again,
I came so that all may have life."

7DAYS:
DAY FIVE

Faith

7 DAYS:
DAY SIX

Victory

7 DAYS:
DAY SEVEN

On day five I heard the words, "No need to write down a bunch of words. One will do, as you are to spend time thinking through the meaning of it. How much time you are to think through this word will be left up to you. During the course of this time during which you're reflecting on this word, it should be long enough, so that you can: then see your own image in the meaning of this word: Faith."

The definition of faith that I came up with, would lead me to day six, and the word for that day which was revealed: Victory.

Now, on day seven, I will share with you what I find not only to be the truth for myself, but also words of wisdom, as they have been so graciously given to me by God, Himself.

By me taking the time out of my life for the last Seven Days, I was able to break through some of the barriers that were created in, and of, my own mind-set. I was able to reflect on them, and compare them to the thoughts and ideas that God would have me to know. By doing so, I was able to walk across the threshold of God's express purpose for myself ever having been assigned to this task that He would ask of myself.

Every individual, at some point in his or her life, has or will have found themselves in the same place that I have found myself at this past week, asking themselves and God above this very question:

Who are they, and what is their express purpose, in life?

I myself when asking this question learned such: I learned that it shall be by my faith in God alone, that I shall receive my victory! That no matter what victory I triumph over, that it would be through my faith in God that I will ever be able to see, or complete any.

So for all whom are the "ye of little faith" or have none at all, I would ask the same of you that was asked of me. I would ask you to spend the next seven days listening to God, and all that He has to say to you. Reflect on what He is speaking to you on, in your life. Then ask God at the end of day four, leaving day's five and six blank, just as I have, ask Him for the two word's He would place on your heart; to stir up the necessary change in you, that would bring forth the permanent fix, and not a temporary fix for yourself.

Once you have been given the two words that God will certainly reveal to you, then go back and fill in the blanks that you have left on those pages, and reveal them to a friend. Explain to them just how much of an influence God is to you, and over your life!

God is the Almighty Influence:
And, I've learned that we can all be too,
if we all do our equal share of the footwork,
by passing on the legacy
of all that we have learned.

< 195 >

THE END

After you've said all that you've had to say,
and done all that God has asked you to do...

Then, God has spoken, and has had His Way...

This book is my testimony of the
work that God willed for me, and appointed me to do.

Not by my will, Lord, but by Yours!

< 196 >

ABOUT THE AUTHOR

Davida Coleman is a native-born New Yorker, who was raised back east in Connecticut before relocating to California some years ago. She is a mother and grandmother, and has served as a mother figure to so many others, over the years. She is very active in her community, as she loves serving others. As a spiritual advisor. Her published works sends her readers on a spell-binding spiritual Journey.

THE BEGINNING AND THE END

Synopsis

Davida Coleman's lint collection of poetry, AS IT WAS IN THE BEGINNING, SO SHALL IT BE IN THE END, is a powerful and emotional walk through her own experiences. She masterfully portrays the parallels she draws to the struggles she bas and those in the lives of others. Generational complications are examined through honest and thought-provoking imagery. Coleman chaperons her readers on a trip through a spiritual enlightenment. She boldly includes life lessons; discussions on the power of learning through and from pain, recognizing the silver linings of our tribulations, showing gratitude for every ounce of good, and celebrating every minute of life we are blessed with. Davida Coleman's reflections on her childhood, her own parenting, and her spiritual journey will inspire readers of all walks of life. This author's thematic approach, highlighting the contrasts between traditional family and spiritual expectations, against her own self-realization, will evoke empathy in and inspire all who read her work.

About the Author

Davida Coleman is a native-born N6w Yorker and a long-time resident of Connecticut. She has three biological children, she's a grandmother of two and is a mother figure- for so many, over the years. She is also very active in her community as she loves serving others as both a Life Coach and a Spiritual Advisor. Her published work sends her readers on a spell-binding spiritual journey.

www.ingramcontent.com/pod-product-compliance
Lightning Source LLC
Chambersburg PA
CBHW061744120626
46550CB00005B/1884